A Second Wind

A Second Wind

Philippe Pozzo di Borgo

Translated by Will Hobson

ATRIA PAPERBACK

New York • London • Toronto • Sydney • New Delhi

ATRIA
PAPERBACK

An Imprint of Simon & Schuster, Inc.
1230 Avenue of the Americas
New York, NY 10020

This Atria Paperback edition February 2018

ATRIA PAPERBACK and colophon are trademarks of Simon & Schuster, Inc.

For information about special discounts for bulk purchases, please contact Simon & Schuster Special Sales at 1-866-506-1949 or business@simonandschuster.com.

The Simon & Schuster Speakers Bureau can bring authors to your live event. For more information or to book an event contact the Simon & Schuster Speakers Bureau at 1-866-248-3049 or visit our website at www.simonspeakers.com.

Designed by Dana Sloan

Manufactured in the United States of America

10 9 8 7 6 5 4 3 2 1

ISBN 978-1-5011-9333-0
ISBN 978-1-4516-8971-6 (ebook)

For my children,
"so the work can go on"

Contents

A Second Wind

Memories Unbound

THE FAULT LINE running through my bones, through my every breath, may be the day of the accident: on June 23, 1993, I became paralyzed. But then on May 3, 1996, St. Philip's Day, Béatrice died. So now I have no past, I have no claim to the future, I am just this pain that I feel at every moment. Béatrice has been stripped back in the same way, reduced to this ever-present feeling of loss. And yet there is a future, that of our two children, Laetitia and Robert-Jean.

Until the accident, I was someone in the world, anxious to leave my mark on events, to make things; since then I have become prey to endless thoughts and, since Béatrice died, to endless grief.

Shadowy memories emerged from these ruins, vague recollections, which at first the pain of paralysis and of mourning would blur during my caffeine-fueled nights. Searching deep within myself, I found the likenesses of the people I'd lost. Then my long, silent vigils started to bring back long-forgotten moments of happiness. My life flowed past me in a stream of images.

I couldn't speak for the first few months after the accident because I'd had a tracheostomy—trach for short—an operation to insert a breathing tube into my windpipe so I could be put on a ventilator. A friend installed a computer and rigged up a set of controls for me under my chin. The alphabet constantly scrolled past on the screen; whenever I stopped the cursor, it would pick out a letter. Slowly these would coalesce to form a word, a sentence, half a page. I loved choosing the right word, the exhausting effort required to type it, the need for precision. Every letter had its own weight, mooring what I wrote like an anchor. I loved the meticulousness of it all. And I had a comrade in arms, Jean-Dominique Bauby, the author of *The Diving Bell and the Butterfly,* who wrote by blinking and died when he reached the last letter.

My own words strangle me when I think of anyone who has died alone, without being able to speak or bear witness or feel any hope.

Lying on my bed at night, I sleep badly. I am paralyzed, after all. After a while, once the trach tube was removed and I could speak again, they put a tape recorder on my stomach. It stops when it can't hear anything—or when it feels like it—and doesn't start again until something new has been said. I never know if I've been recorded. Often I'm stumped for words anyway. It's hard telling a story when you're not sitting at a desk with a piece of paper in front of you and your forehead propped in your left hand, when you can't just let it rip, scribble away and cross things out or start again, when there's only the voice of someone who could be dead and a tape deck irrevocably recording what you say, with no room for second thoughts, no crossings out. The snapshots of a faltering memory . . .

I've lost the thread now. It's dark and I hurt all over. My shoulders hunch up and I feel a shooting pain on the top of the right one, as if I've been stabbed. I have to stop. My cat, F-sharp, is having a lovely time clambering all over my body that is quivering and arching backward as if beseeching God for something. Spasming and shaking, suddenly it's all too much for me, tears well up. The cat, as usual, is a picture of blithe indifference. It spends the whole night playing around on top of me, as if it needs my convulsive shudders to feel alive.

The subcutaneous fire burning continuously from my shoulders to the tips of my fingers and toes is all too liable to blaze up at any moment. From the burning in my body I can tell if it's going to be fine tomorrow or rain. I feel scalding, corrosive pain in my hands, my buttocks, down my thighs, around my knees, at the base of my calves.

They quarter me, stretching out my arms and legs in the hope it will bring me some relief, but the pain doesn't let up. They call it phantom pain. Phantom my ass! I cry because I'm in pain, not because I'm sad. I wait for the tears to give me some respite, until I've cried myself into a stupor.

We used to make love at night by candlelight, whispering

to each other. She'd fall asleep in the early hours in the crook of my neck. I still talk to her.

Sometimes, sick with loneliness, I turn to Flavia, a film student. She has a beaming smile, a sumptuous mouth, a quizzical left eyebrow. When she stands with her back to the window in her flowing, light blue dress, she doesn't realize she might as well be wearing nothing, that her twenty-seven-year-old frame can still arouse a phantom. I let her transcribe everything, I have no decency, she is transparent.

The cat comes back to sit on my stomach. When he changes position, my body tenses as if it's revolted by him being here and not Béatrice.

I have to talk about the good times though, I have to forget the suffering. Why not start with the final moments of my life, my foreseeable and sometimes longed-for death that will reunite me with Béatrice. I will leave the ones I love to be with the one I have loved so much. Even if her paradise doesn't exist, I trust that's where she will be because she believed in it. Because that's what I want. Freed from all our suffering, we'll be together there, cocooned in each other's arms, our eyes closed for eternity. A rustle of silken wings, Béatrice's blond hair stirs. . . .

Béatrice, who art in Heaven, save me.

My Senses

I WAS SOMEBODY ONCE. Now I'm paralyzed, I've lost almost all sensation in my body. But even so, somewhere among the excruciating pain, there are still delicious memories of the senses that have abandoned me.

Retrieving my shattered body's experiences, inch by inch, memory by memory, is a form of survival. Working back from my current immobility, putting a chaotic mass of short-lived sensations into some sort of chronological order, helps me to reclaim my past and reconnect my two entirely separate lives.

*

A FLUSH of confusion sets my whole body aglow. It's only a memory. Even so I feel drowsy, my rational mind is shutting down, I am overwhelmed by far-off sensations, from when I was seven, or perhaps eight, and the dazzling Casablanca sun was beating down . . . My brothers and I were at the Collège Charles de Foucauld, a church school. At recess some of my classmates would play football in the middle of the playground, raising a film of dust that would stick to their arms and legs, and turn their shorts and navy blue shirts milky white. Others, aficionados of a local version of marbles played with apricot stones, would gather by the walls in groups of shopkeepers and players. I was a shopkeeper; Alain—my twin brother who was a crack shot—was a player. The shopkeeper would place an apricot stone between his legs and the player would try to hit it with his trusty projectile. I took up position by the playground wall, facing the morning sun—I loved baking myself to a crisp in the sun—and waited for Alain to throw, my half-closed eyes fixed on my stone. I counted to three, then shivered with pleasure. Drowsy from the warm, dusty playground, I drifted off. When I came to, my class had gone back inside; the playground was full of children I didn't recognize. I shot bolt upright in a panic, wrapped my supply of apricot stones in a handkerchief, and ran back as fast as I could, my body on fire. For the first time, I felt a strange warmth between my legs. Was it the shorts rubbing or fear of my horrible schoolmistress? Either way, something was happening down there. I knocked frantically, the schoolmistress barked out a command, I pushed open the door, and then just stood there, motionless.

*

I FLUSH bright red all over again, alone in my bed, as I remember these first stirrings of desire.

*

NOT LONG afterward, we were in Holland. My father was working for an Anglo-Dutch oil company. My brothers Reynier and Alain; Valerie, my little sister; Christina, the governess; and I all slept on the first floor. Christina was very beautiful with her red hair and green eyes and freckles, which I kept discovering all over her body, helped by the fact that it was the heyday of the miniskirt. One day she was doing some ironing on the landing. I had been hanging around watching her for ages, when I felt that discomfort under my belt again. I blushed, not daring to look down at my gray flannel English shorts. Oh no, what was Christina doing? Squinting to see what was going on? I was done for. Until she—the beautiful, treacherous girl—did something extraordinary. She stepped out from behind the ironing board, came toward me, turned round, and bent over as far as she could. Was it really because she needed to pick something up?

If I'd known how and been able to, I would have taken her there and then. But I just stood there breathlessly, arms dangling, everything else straining skyward. I seemed to look at her bottom for an eternity.

Years later I saw some photos of her. I didn't find her such a beauty that time, with her gappy teeth, double chin, and bony knees. Everything is a matter of perspective . . .

*

AT NIGHT I take deep breaths to try to free myself from the pain that alienates me from everything. Images come into my mind—so concrete and simple, I find them very beautiful— but the pain doesn't abate.

*

I WAS fifteen and I wanted to impress my friends, so I went into the drug store. When it was my turn, I said, "Can I have a packet," my voice fell to a whisper, "of condoms?" The female chemist asked me to repeat myself. Trapped, already bright red in the face, I asked her again. In a gently ironic tone, she then inquired, "Small, medium, or large?" I ran out the door.

Naturally she was talking about the size of the packet.

*

A LAUGH bubbles up in my throat and is answered by a spasm, which knocks the tape recorder off my chest. I have to start again, rebuild my world. I call Abdel, my caregiver. He puts the tape recorder back in position, and my strange, muffled voice sets it in motion. The voice I have now not only sounds completely different to "my" voice, but also changes constantly, as if my identity has gone to pieces like my body. My chest muscles don't work anymore, so I can't convey intonation or punctuation; the tape only registers the bare information of whatever words I have enough breath to utter.

*

I WAS seventeen, and we were on a skiing holiday. Alain already had his "squeeze." We spent our time on the slopes with boys, and with girls, and I'd never blushed so much in my life as when I was with the latter. One night after supper we all crowded in by the fire, drinking wine, singing, playing guitar. I was next to a girl. She leaned over at one point and rested her head on my shoulder. A friend of Alain's girlfriend, she was older than me and had been born in Vietnam to a French colonial family. She had slanting eyes and olive skin. She laughed, then moved closer. I could smell her spicy scent now. I tried to shrink into the fireplace, but that didn't change anything. I could feel desire burning in me; I wanted her. When it was time for bed and she led me to the only single room and to a little bed by the wall, I followed without a backward glance. I'd been dreaming of that moment for years, it felt like. She unceremoniously took off her clothes and lay on top of me. I must have seemed awkward because she smiled, then burst out laughing: "You haven't taken off your pants!" She helped me. We were together for a few months.

*

EVEN NOW that I'm paralyzed, my inert senses can still play tricks on me, as they did early on during my time at Kerpape, a rehabilitation center on the Brittany coast. For my first outing, Béatrice pushed my new wheelchair to a little café by the sea and sat opposite me. Over her shoulder, windsurfers leaped the waves. The sky was gray. My neck felt clammy with sweat, but it was so lovely having Béatrice's face close to mine, I didn't want to break the spell. How could she still have that look of young love in her eyes as she gazed at the shadow of the man she had fallen for? After a while, I broke into a hacking cough. Béatrice became worried and took me back to the rehab center. The nurse diagnosed a lung infection, so I was returned to intensive care at the hospital in Lorient for the second time. My throat was opened up by another trach, an array of bottles decanted their poisons into me, while Béatrice sat by my bed. The veins in my left arm couldn't cope after a while, so they bandaged it up to the elbow in cotton wool soaked in alcohol. I soon felt drunk. My room didn't have a window, but I guessed it was nighttime. There was no nurse in sight. The red, green, and white lights of the machines blinked on and off. I was drifting farther and farther away, when suddenly a wildly pleasurable sensation came over me. I hadn't felt intense desire for Béatrice for a year. Images of our bodies together raced through my mind. Suddenly the lights came on in a blinding flash of neon. Béatrice was bending over me. She'd understood immediately what was happening when she saw my eyelids fluttering. I asked her to tell the doctor. Laughing, she ran out into the corridor. The doctor came back with her, an irritated look on his face. He examined the object of these mad giggles. Negative. Phantom stirrings. Go back to sleep, my angel.

The Angel's Luck

THE DAY BEGINS with DRE, then the shower.[1] Everything's dark. I seem barely to exist. I don't have a body, there's no sound, no sensations, other than perhaps a faint awareness of warm air wafting into my nostrils. Then suddenly it all changes and we're off again. My head slumps forward. I hear the water of the shower and feel it on my face. I open my eyes and gradually an image materializes—of Marcelle, the soft-voiced giant from Martinique, who has got my legs on her shoulders. "Ah M. Pozzo, we're back, are we? I didn't have to slap you this time." My right arm has slipped off its rest, so I'm slumped over on the side of my shower seat, a miser-

---

1   DRE: Digital rectal examination. Stage two of my morning routine, after emptying my urine bag, is to roll me onto my side, put on a glove, apply cream to the index finger, and put it you know where. I know I was born lucky but this does seem to be taking the principle a bit far. I shut my eyes as the nurses rootle around. Thank you to everyone—Marcelle, Berthe, Pauline, Catherine, Isabelle, Sabrya, and Sandrine—for your light touch and your kindness. I am that rare thing, someone who can be kept alive with the tip of an index finger.

able object with holes in it. I am virtually naked, apart from a urine bag, which is attached to my penis by a long tube and something like a condom. In English it's known as a condom catheter, whereas in France, its brand name, Pénilex, brings to my mind *"pénible,"* which means "painful," apart from anything else, although its etymology is probably *"pénis,"* or the apology for one in my case.

I can't sit up by myself. If an ounce of blood is to remain in my brain, I need to be trussed up in a huge abdominal belt and covered in thick compression stockings from my toes to my buttocks. When I faint, as I often do, I become an angel of darkness, an angel that feels nothing. When I return to the light with my legs in the air, pain courses through me whether I have been slapped or not, and the dazzling brightness of this hell makes me cry.

Marcelle calls in Abdel to lift me onto the bed. He unhooks my feet from the footrests, bends down until his head is touching my chest, wedges my knees between his, wraps his sturdy arms around my lower back, and . . . one, two, three . . . He leans backward and I find myself on my feet looking at my reflection in the still-closed shutters. There was a time in my life when I was good-looking, but there's little sign of that now. All the blood rushes to my toes, I become an angel again, until Abdel lies me down on the pressure sore mattress. Marcelle starts what she calls with a smile "the intimate ablutions." She takes off the Pénilex to tend to the beast. Béatrice used to call it Toto affectionately.

I hear Marcelle laugh. Toto has become erect. She can't get the Pénilex back on.

THE QUADRIPLEGICS were the aristocracy in Kerpape rehabilitation center. We were the flower of society, so close to God that naturally we looked down on everyone else. We were the quads! But when we were on our own, we'd call ourselves the "tads," because a tadpole, like a quad, doesn't have arms or legs, just a wriggling cock.

Part One

Gilded Childhood

I Was Born . . .

As THE DESCENDANT of the Dukes of Pozzo di Borgo and the Marquis de Vogüé, to say I was born lucky is putting it mildly.

During the Reign of Terror, Carl-Andrea Pozzo di Borgo parted ways with his erstwhile friend Napoleon. While he was still very young, Pozzo di Borgo became prime minister of Corsica under British protection, was forced into exile in Russia, and from there—thanks to his knowledge of the "Ogre"— played his part in the monarchies' victory. Whereupon he set about amassing a fortune by putting a very high price on the considerable influence he had with the tsar. Dukes, counts, and all the other European nobles swept aside by the French Revolution thanked him handsomely when he helped them to recover their properties and positions. Louis XVIII went so far as to say that Pozzo "was the one who cost him the most." Through judicious alliances, the Pozzos have handed down this family dough from generation to generation until the present. You can still hear people in the Corsican mountains say that someone is as "rich as a Pozzo."

Joseph, or "Joe" as he preferred, Duke of Pozzo di Borgo, my grandfather, married an American gold mine, whose grandchildren called her by the English epithet "Granny." Grandpapa Joe used to relish telling the story of how they got married in 1923. Granny was twenty and had embarked with her mother on a grand tour of Europe to meet the continent's most eligible bachelors. The two women arrived at the Château de Dangu in Normandy to stay with a Corsican, who turned out to be a head shorter than Granny. Addressing her daughter across the vast dining room table at lunch, Granny's mother remarked in English (which of course everyone understood), "Don't you think the duke we saw yesterday had a much prettier château, dear?" This didn't, however, prevent Granny from choosing the little Corsican over his rival.

When the Left came to power in 1936, Joe Pozzo di Borgo was imprisoned for membership in La Cagoule, an extreme right-wing organization that was hell-bent on overthrowing the Third Republic, even though he wasn't remotely in sympathy with them. During his stay in La Santé prison, he was visited by his wife and a select group of friends. "The awkward thing about being in prison when people want to see you," he joked, "is that you can't send someone to say you're not in."

The Corsican Perfettini clan, who had defended our interests on the island since our exile to Russia, were outraged by grandfather's plight. A delegation went to Paris armed to

the teeth and descended on La Santé. Philippe, the Perfettini patriarch, asked the duke for a hit list so they could mete
out retribution, only to be advised by Grandfather to go home
quietly. On his way out, old Philippe, surprised and disap-
pointed, anxiously asked the duchess, "Is the duke tired?"

Grandfather stopped playing an active role in politics after
that and withdrew to his properties: the Parisian town house,
the Norman château, the Corsican mountain, and the Dario
Palace in Venice. There he held court to a brilliant circle of
friends; a center of opposition no matter who was in power.
He died when I was fifteen. I can't think I was ever won over
by any of his flights of oratory, dazzling though they were.
They seemed to be from another age. But I do remember a
party in Paris, when their ballroom was aglitter with dia-
monds. I was a child. My head came up to the "posteriors" of
the glamorous crowd. At one point, to my perplexity, I spotted
my dear grandfather's hand resting on a generously uphol-
stered behind, which did not belong to his lawfully wedded
wife.

The Vogüé family's origins, meanwhile, are lost in the
mists of time. As grandfather Pozzo said to grandfather
Vogüé (the two patriarchs loathed each other): "At least our
titles are recent enough for us to prove they're genuine!" Robert-Jean de Vogüé didn't rise to the bait.

Grandfather Vogüé, who was a regular officer, fought in
both world wars: he was seventeen in the first, and an N.N.
political prisoner in Ziegenhain during the second. N.N.—

"Nacht und Nebel" (Night and Fog)—was a Nazi directive in 1941 whereby prisoners were secretly transported to Germany and all knowledge of them was denied to their relatives; in most cases they did not return alive. He was a brave man with deeply felt convictions. Loyal to the code of his knightly ancestors, he saw his family's inherited privileges as compensation for its services to society: in the Middle Ages, to its defense; in the twentieth century, to its economic development. He married the most beautiful girl of her generation, one of the Moët & Chandon heiresses, and in the 1920s left the army to join the champagne company, which he subsequently ran—and expanded hugely—until his retirement in 1973. In his hands, a small family concern grew into an empire.

These remarkable achievements were the product not only of his strength of character but also his political convictions, which he gathered together at the end of his life in a small book titled, *Alerte aux patrons!* (*A Warning to Employers!*) (1974). It is still on my bedside table.

As might be expected, Robert-Jean de Vogüé was heavily criticized by his peers for throwing in his lot so emphatically with the workers. He was even called "the red marquis," to which his reply was "I am not a marquis, I am a count." He let them think what they liked about his political allegiances. The financiers who succeeded him destroyed his work. He remains my mentor to this day. Our son is named Robert-Jean after him.

My father, Charles-André, was the eldest of Joe Pozzo di

Borgo's children. He decided to go to work to prove himself. There is an argument, in fact, to say he was the first Pozzo to have a job. It was his way of standing up to his father. He started working on the oil fields in North Africa, then built a career in the oil business through industriousness, enterprise, and consummate efficiency. His professional life took him all over the world, and I followed from an early age. A few years after his father died—he was running an oil company at the time—he put his career on hold to sort out the family's affairs.

My dear mother had three children in one year: first my older brother Reynier, then me and my twin, Alain, eleven months later. She moved fifteen times during my father's career, always leaving behind large amounts of bulky furniture and the few friends she'd been able to acquire. As we traveled constantly, she had a nanny to protect her from the worst of our unruliness. I had a habit, for instance, of sitting on Alain when we shared a stroller. He waited many years—and until he was a couple of inches taller than me—before giving me a thrashing that relieved a modicum of his pent-up frustration.

*

NOWADAYS HE pushes me about like a hunchback in my wheelchair. They all tower over me. I refuse to look up.

*

IN TRINIDAD, we spent all our time on the beach, dressed like the locals with whom we swam and played from dusk till dawn. We learned to express ourselves in patois before we could even speak French. In the evening we'd fight in our room. I have a vivid memory of one game, which involved jumping up and down on your bed while pissing on your neighbor's. North Africa was next: Algeria and Morocco. We discovered school, learned French from a spinster of indeterminate age—a shy, still girlish woman. One day there was a high wind, and as I clung to a telephone pole I saw my puny brother being blown away. Mademoiselle tried to hang on to him, without success. A fence stopped them. For the first time I felt a twinge of jealousy for this twin of mine, who was getting a woman's full attention.

*

NOW I am a good five feet nine. One hundred and twelve pounds of inert matter, the rest deadweight. No use to anyone.

*

REYNIER QUICKLY distanced himself from us. We gave him an English nickname, Big Fat. Soon the only show in town was *The Twins vs. Big Fat, the Enforcer.* Keenly aware of his responsibilities as heir, our elder brother wouldn't hesitate to use his height advantage to pummel us with his platelike hands whenever he felt we needed to be taught a lesson.

*

NOW I am pitiful and cry and can't hit the people who take advantage of my paralysis.

*

AFTER MOROCCO came London. The nanny this time was called Nancy. I noticed Reynier had a little game he'd play with this beautiful brunette. He'd slip into her bed without my parents knowing and I'd hear him chuckling in there. Without really knowing why, I tried everything I could think of to get into Nancy's bed. I even tried to catch a fever once by sitting on a boiling hot radiator. I figured that if Nancy would look after me, maybe I'd end up in her bed. . . . The attempt was short-lived. I had a traitor in the ranks, my bottom. With my buttocks and cheeks on fire, I had to lift the siege.

*

I MISS the sensations that used to prove where I ended and the world began. This body, with its unfathomable boundaries, doesn't belong to me anymore. Even if someone wants to caress me, their hand never touches me. But these images still move me, despite the fact that I am constantly on fire now.

. . . *Lucky*

W HEN I WAS eight, my two brothers and I were summoned to Granny's house in Paris. She was a talented violinist but hadn't been able to keep it up after she married, since Joe the duke didn't have any time for "that noise." Her prized possessions were a small, elegant violin and a wonderful Steinway. She lined up the three of us in the ballroom. I immediately laid claim to the huge black piano, which fascinated me. Alain was bowled over by the diminutive violin and its complexity. Whereas Reynier, when he couldn't see any more instruments on offer, lost interest in music from then on, which meant he'd have plenty of opportunities in the future to loudly mock Alain's and my attempts to play duets. It must have been agony having to listen to us. I can still remember the humiliation of a concert Alain and I gave at his boarding school. It was a Beethoven sonatina, Alain played the violin, I accompanied him on piano. He began the piece at one side of the stage and ended it, to loud boos from his schoolmates, at the other. I never played in public after that. I don't play at all now.

Granny put on many wonderful concerts in that ballroom in Paris, and I was always in the front row. Later she organized a music festival in the Château de la Punta above Ajaccio. Béatrice was in charge of publicity, while I plastered posters all over Corsica.

The château was a museum dedicated to the life of Carl-Andrea Pozzo di Borgo. I remember the attendant who used to show visitors around the lavish reception rooms, library, and bedrooms. Two large paintings faced each other in the library: one of Carl-Andrea Pozzo di Borgo in majesty, at the height of his triumph, painted by Baron François Gérard; the other was of Napoleon just before he left for Elba, his face scarred with disappointment and bitterness, painted by Jacques-Louis David. After an exhaustive tour, the fount of knowledge would conclude by saying in a Corsican accent thick enough to cut with a knife, "And the toilets are of the period, too. Don't forget the guide!"

A Pozzo had never lived in the château. One of our ancestors had built it to entice his wife to live on the island. He bought the stones from the Marie de' Medici pavilion, which had formed part of the outer wall of the Tuileries Palace until the Commune fire in 1871. After a brief stay in Ajaccio and a night in the château, however, his bride categorically refused ever to set foot on the island again. It had become fairly dilapi-

dated, but Grandfather Joe preferred to restore an old Genoese tower about two hundred yards above it, in the heart of
what used to be the village of Pozzo di Borgo. He loved staying there with Granny. Time seemed amazingly palpable to
him when he looked out of the tower to see a chapel on the
mountainside in which every member of our family is buried,
as Granny, the Duchess of Pozzo di Borgo and Joe's faithful
wife, will be in time too. And as I will be with Béatrice.

MY FATHER formed a clear-cut idea of each of his children
at a very early age. Despite his profound kindness, he delivered these judgements with brutal honesty. They were always
brief. "Reynier isn't academic." So Reynier was sent to board at
the École des Roches. It was the only English-style boarding
school in France. The older boys were in charge of teaching
the younger ones to take responsibility for themselves; prece-
dence was given to sport over intellectual pursuits in general.
Reynier didn't excel as a student there and never acquired a
taste for sport, but he did develop a passion for drawing, inherited from our mother. Alain followed in Reynier's footsteps
at Les Roches. "Maybe he'll do something there." Our father
took a long time to make up his mind about my twin brother's
intellectual capacities, partly, perhaps, because he was virtually mute. And I, finally, was launched on the path my father
and his father had taken because I was "the least stupid of the
three." I was eight when he took me to Paris to sit the entrance

exam for the Lycée Montaigne. The day the results came out, my father held my hand as he looked for our name on the list. I was entitled to a "Good." I'd gotten in. And so the moment came for me to leave my family. From then on I could only see them during school holidays.

Éliane de Compiègne, my father's sister, lived in the family town house in Paris with her husband Philippe and their three children. I stayed with them every weekend and spent Thursday afternoons there too. I'd take the bus from the Jardin du Luxembourg and, whenever I could, I'd stand on the platform at the back. That was my favorite thing in the world, watching the streets roll past in the haze and the exhaust fumes as the conductor leaned nonchalantly on the rail, his cap pushed back on his head, his hand hovering over the stop bell. The Compiègnes became my second family. They put me under the eaves, in the laundry. I slept in a bed that folded out of a cupboard. I discovered a completely different France.

Philippe de Compiègne could have been among the entourage of Bertrand du Guesclin, the Breton knight and hero of the Hundred Years' War; his family certainly date from that period. He had a noble warrior's nature and was a wonderful hunter. After his marriage, he divided his time between Paris, where he ran a small factory making luxury packaging, and La Chaise, his impoverished seigneury, which consisted of the remains of a hamlet clinging to a ruined château. He managed to deck out a few of the château's rooms to create something reminiscent of an animal's lair, but the greater part of his time was spent hunting in the seven square miles of forest that constituted his fiefdom. He died surrounded by his beloved animals, having stubbornly refused to take care of his health to the end.

He taught me to hunt and gave me a taste for long hours stalking, alone among the trees. He also taught me fly-fishing, another solitary sport, in which everything depended on sharp-sightedness and the elegance of one's movements. Uncle Philippe didn't talk much. Sometimes, in fact, he let his fists make his point. Once the gamekeeper in Normandy found himself sprawled in his lettuces, laid out by an upper-cut. My uncle thought this charming fellow was guilty of a lack of respect to his mother-in-law, the duchess. A pretentious socialite also bore the brunt of his temper. His aristocratic truculence made it impossible for him to bear the stupidity of his peers.

When he wasn't hunting, he saw his circle of fifteen faithful friends, never more, always the same faces. They met up at least once a week at the Pozzo town house to "shuffle the deck." A spirit of pure brotherly feeling reigned. If one of them became besotted with a woman who wasn't his wife, for instance, the matter was conducted with the greatest sensitivity and kindness. Their furious games of gin rummy started at about five in the afternoon. Facing one another across a long, narrow table, two rows of five to six players went at it until late into the night. They stopped to eat at eight, and dinner always revolved around Aunt Éliane, who had a knack for telling the raunchiest stories with an air of innocent incomprehension. I've never laughed as much as I did with that family and their group of friends. Their parties were an unfailing joy in that part of my adolescence. Aunt Éliane wasted no time initiating me into the mysteries of gin rummy and I became a good partner. I have liked cards ever since. The Compiègnes introduced me to a fine selection of life's pleasures, a compound of equal parts insouciance, deep friendship, and elegance of mind. It was a very special atmosphere, at once tough-minded and sensitive.

Their eldest son, François, who was two years younger than me, was my playmate throughout our teenage years. A great brute, like all the Compiègnes, he was also unbelievably clumsy. He must have about a hundred stitches by now. I still remember cycling through the woods in Dangu. I would forge ahead, tearing down the hillside through the trees, and then have to stop to pick up François because he'd fallen off and cut himself to ribbons. He hasn't changed a bit; he's still the same fragile force of nature as an adult.

*

ONE DAY I went off the rails. I discovered solitude. From then on I actively sought it out. I always wanted to go faster, farther, higher. I felt immortal. Even the avalanche I was caught in at Les Arcs didn't leave a scar. I came off the road countless times, and yet I'd just set off again without batting an eyelid. But I missed a step. I still can't remember the moment my earthbound condition caught up with me.

*

WHEN FRANÇOIS was twelve, Uncle Philippe gave him one of
the post office's orangey-yellow Citroën 2CV, which he had
bought at a government auction. Good old Titine, as we called
the car, was our playmate for several years. At age fourteen, I
was tearing around the muddy tracks in the woods, skidding
wildly around the corners. I have since found pictures of that
car: they show us as the teenagers we were, posing trium-
phantly around our "tank," hands in pockets, cigarettes in
mouths. The world belonged to us. We were spoiled children.

My uncle Cecco, my father's younger brother, and his
wife Tania, an actress whose screen name was Odile Ver-
sois, would also stay in the family town house on occasion.
When they did, I had a bird's-eye view from my window into
the room of the sylph who looked after their children. For
three years this governess was the most beautiful woman in
the world to me. I would glimpse her silhouette through the
frosted glass of the bathroom window and then dream about
her all night. One evening, crazed with desire, I tiptoed down
the two flights of stairs that separated us, crept along the passage and into her bedroom, which was at the very end. She
was about to get into bed. I could see her body through her
nightie. I just stood there, embarrassed and overcome. Finally, unbelievably sheepishly, I said I had a headache. She
gave me an aspirin. Then I went back upstairs, with my tail
between my legs.

While studying in Paris, my weeknights were spent at the École Bossuet, a boarding school run by black-clad monks. We had mass there every morning, ate our meals in the cafeteria, and had supervised study periods in the evening. We attended classes first at the Lycée Montaigne, then at the Lycée Louis-le-Grand. From time to time I would serve as an unenthusiastic altar boy.

One morning I stole all the unconsecrated hosts with a few friends. We polished them off by the time we got back to our pew. Total success when the old canon came to celebrate the Eucharist . . . Detention all around.

Bossuet's father superior, Canon Garand, was over eighty. He had taught my grandfather, no less. He was already headmaster when my father had been there. One day I went up to the seventh floor and, standing at a window armed with a water balloon and surrounded by my friends, I lined him up in my sights. He was crossing the courtyard, perhaps having just meditated on the unknowability of life. *Hisss . . . splat!* The missile described a perfect trajectory and burst, soaking his cassock. Mission accomplished!

When he heard of my "exploit," my father didn't raise any objection to my being expelled. In fact, he had already decided to move me from Bossuet, having found out that I spent most of my time in a café where I was nicknamed the King of Pinball. I was sent to the École des Roches, where I was reunited with my brothers.

I arrived at the end of the sixth year, aged sixteen, and instantly took against the politics of the place. The fees meant that the school's intake was limited to the financial elite, but the postwar boom had allowed for a new, incredibly wealthy, crass type of pupil. I remember repulsive brats being driven everywhere by chauffeurs. One even made his entrance into the huge park in an old Rolls-Royce with a liveried servant standing on the running board! I felt ashamed for him and for myself. I hadn't been aware of the concept of class until then.

I cut myself off from everyone in the school, hardly saw my brothers, spent hours playing the piano or chain-smoking in my study cubicle.

*

LATER IN life, oppressed by social injustice, I have gone to extreme lengths to ensure that at least the people I'm responsible for are capable of being independent.

When we were asked to fire hundreds of people, I was ready to take up arms in protest. Trembling with indignation, surrounded by the glacial laws of the economy, I would probably have turned any weapons on myself so they couldn't take me alive.

*

I DISCOVERED Karl Marx, Friedrich Engels, Louis Althusser. In my room, I studied these "red" thinkers while listening to

Twenty Contemplations of the Infant Jesus, Olivier Messiaen's pieces for piano. The music insulated me from my corrupt environment. I was in such a violent state of revolt that I refused to attend any school gatherings. At an awards ceremony, I received a prize in absentia. That was a first in the school's history.

Since the accident, I've remembered something that barely registered at the time. Our mathematics teacher, M. Mortas, died in a car crash. A rumor went around that he had grown eight inches taller after being run over by a tractor. I remember this now that I'm prone, which apparently, so everyone tells me, makes me look taller.

May 1968 found me in that anachronistic establishment. I decided to run away to Paris where I was swept up in the tide of enthusiasm that reigned from the Odéon to the Panthéon. I was convinced those crazy days would lead to more justice in the world, that decency and respect would govern human relations from then on. I floated around, my feet not touching the ground, intoxicated by the excitement and gunpowder, with no preconceived ideas other than that a fraternal, romantic age was about to be ushered in. I spent my nights with old school friends from Louis-le-Grand, debating into the early hours the ways we were going to improve society.

*

I REFUSE to compromise, to be another craven idiot of these modern times!

Mother "of a Thousand Smiles"

MY FATHER BOUGHT a forty-foot boat. I was ten the first time we sailed to Corsica. My mother came with us, even though she was terrified by the elements. She would become her usual calm self again when we put in at one of the ports of the "sea of a thousand smiles," as Socrates referred to the Mediterranean.

One summer we made the crossing in a strong mistral. The sea was white with spray and waves crashed onto the boat's canoe stern before dropping into the cockpit. My father put up a storm jib and held his course. As we neared Calvi, I managed to get to my feet and extricate myself from the noxious-smelling huddle of my siblings in the cabin. We made a triumphant entrance into the port, proudly crowding around our father as he drew alongside the quay. People looked on dumbfounded at this crazy vessel emerging from the eye of the storm, particularly because my father had insisted we come in under sail.

Each year, the distances grew. We explored all of Corsica and Sardinia, Elba, the Italian coast, and finally the Ionian Sea, including the island of Zante. We found a cemetery containing the graves of fifty of our ancestors, who had been hired as mercenaries by the doges of Venice. This branch of our family had died out in an attack by the Turks. An attendant at the cemetery maintained their graves, for no apparent reason. We spent almost an hour there, observing the procession of two centuries of our relatives. So many lives reduced to a name and a set of dates on a stone. Some lives had been long—we imagined a patriarch proudly taking his rest; others had been short—children who had died young. I came away from this visit with a dizzying sense of time passing, a cadence of generations marching by, all bound together by the common cemetery wall.

Four years later our father bought a bigger boat, a magnificent fiberglass fifty-three-footer with two masts and two cabins. Its wake tracked across huge distances. We set out from La Rochelle, circumnavigated Europe via Gibraltar, ventured deep into the Mediterranean as far as Turkey, and then came back via Portugal.

THESE LONG expeditions had a lasting influence on us boys. My father asserted his authority with terrifying force. Sometimes, when we were in the middle of a tricky maneuver, he would give us a terrible tongue-lashing. Each of us would react in our own way: Alain, white as a sheet, would remain utterly silent; Reynier would blow up and march off, leaving us in the lurch as the storm raged, tears of humiliation streaming down his face; and, in my case, I would be petrified by my father's fearsome rants at first, but then I'd try to work out the reasons for these outbursts. He would have to shout to make himself heard above the roar of the sea and wind. Sometimes the danger was so urgent he'd jump into the cockpit, yelling at us.

I learned about sustained effort when we were at sea, the importance of being humble in the face of the natural elements, but also the art of occasionally thumbing one's nose at them. They were intoxicating, those voyages. Nothing gave me more pleasure than to take the helm with the sails and stars overhead, the white bulk of the ship rushing forward into the darkness in an arc of phosphorescent spray, the waves breaking heavily on the hull and dissolving into champagne bubbles.

One summer, disaster struck. We had set off from Lisbon planning to reach Gibraltar the following day. At three in the morning, the sea had started to rise, but it wasn't dangerous, so we continued under full sail. Reynier was on watch. The bow cut through the seas, the boat raced over the swell at top speed, everything was in order. Then there was a horrific crash, and we were shipwrecked. A lighthouse on the coast hadn't been working, so, without realizing, Reynier had been navigating on another light, which sent us straight onto Cape St. Vincent. Miraculously, we struck a sandy stretch between rocks. The impact was so violent I was catapulted out of my bunk into the sea, but nobody was hurt and the boat lay on the sand without breaking up. In no time, locals came to our rescue, appearing through the early morning mist with their donkeys. They stowed the boat, and while some warmed us up with a roaring fire, others took our belongings off the boat and loaded up their donkeys. We followed the convoy to the village, where they informed the authorities. We stayed with them for two days, the time needed to salvage the boat, and they treated us with the warmest hospitality. Their kindness seemed like a vestige of some sort of original, shared humanity, as if it were a trait that somehow depended on poverty.

*

THINKING BACK to those early, gilded years, I realize I was a spoiled child. I can't resist trying to identify the influences that profoundly marked me. Some are genetic. Physically I am the spitting image of Grandfather Joe. Apparently I've also inherited some of his wit and fondness for the fairer sex. I get my aesthetic sense, or should that be coquetry, and my taste for power from Grandfather Vogüé. When I worked at Moët, his former secretary Marie-Thérèse worked for me and always used to point out resemblances between us. Granny's bequeathed me her puritan morality and American way of thinking. Protestant until her marriage, she always maintained the strict rigor and ascetic tendencies of that religion.

Overall, I'm the product of heredity and my admiration for the way of life of these two great families—one old-fashioned, the other ahead of its time. I am an odd blend of duty toward my surroundings, and detachment from them. A sort of aloof industriousness. And even after the tragic things that have happened, even now that I'm immobile, these are still the driving forces in my life.

Part Two

Béatrice

Renaissance

EVERYTHING BEGAN THE day we met, aged twenty, in a courtyard at the University of Reims Champagne-Ardenne. We were both there by chance: her father had become prefect of the Departement of Marne, so his family had moved with him. My parents had moved abroad, and I'd decided to stay behind to study.

Béatrice and I spent almost all our time at university together. The Law and Economics Faculty at Reims is in an old building, which, at the time, also housed a hospice for the elderly. You turned left at the entrance for the old people and right for the students. In between, there was a chapel, which would be draped in black when a resident on the left departed this world. They'd ruefully watch us go past every morning. Such a huge gulf separated us; they expected nothing, and we hoped for everything.

Politically, the faculty was on the far left in 1969. I hardly ever went to lectures. I spent most of my time in a little café next door. It was run by a recovering alcoholic and his wife, who sported a black wig and an electric pink ensemble. They made sure I drank more lemonade than beer during my mammoth pinball and dice sessions. I would occasionally show up at the college, which was on strike, to raise my hand at one of the general meetings and vote for the protests to continue. Time passed in a dreary, uneventful way. I retook my first year.

I could have loafed around like that my entire time at university if I hadn't noticed a tall, blond girl one day. She stood out because she wasn't wearing the regulation uniform of the time: jeans, tight sweater, and a cigarette. The next day there were more hospice residents at the gate than usual; something was going on. I went into the courtyard. The beautiful girl was there with a few friends, armed with rolls of white paper. She was waylaying students to get them to sign a petition. I went up to this vision. She invited me to add my name to those wanting to stop the strike and, blushing, I did so immediately. Amused, she gave me a roll of paper so I could help collect signatures. From that day on, we never left each other's side. From that day on, my life began.

I used to argue with Béatrice. With no preconceptions about politics, she stood up for whatever struck her as reasonable and laughed at lots of things that I'd always found deadly serious. She saw life as a human comedy; I thought of it as more of a tragedy. We squabbled over these differences but at night she kept me close to her. She soon introduced me to her parents in the lavish prefect's residence. I almost blew everything. Her mother was in her formal garden. Upsa, my dog, took an instant liking to her, bowling her over into the rose bushes and licking her face. Nevertheless, madame suggested that Upsa could be a permanent guest there so that she could have the run of the garden (and so Béatrice wouldn't stray too far). I acquiesced. My eighty-square-foot pad wasn't enough for Upsa, who spent the whole day shut up in it. My jobs as a night watchman and as a door-to-door salesman—selling encyclopedias and suits in the working-class neighborhoods of Reims, Troyes, and Châlons-en-Champagne—didn't leave much time for my studies, let alone for Upsa. From then on we spent every weekend at the prefecture.

I was put in General de Gaulle's room, which boasted a huge bed that had been made to order. Béatrice used to come and join me there late at night and then bring me breakfast in bed in the morning. She was so funny. She thought she was fooling her parents until the day my charming future mother-in-law appeared at the door with a little smile and asked her daughter if she could just have a word with her.

At least half the day would be spent in that bed planning our future. We decided to go in for Sciences-Po (L'Institut d'Études Politiques) and then the ENA (L'École Nationale d'Administration), two of the most competitive graduate schools in France. I finally started to do some work.

I took Béatrice to Corsica in the summer holidays to stay with my family. We were the first of our generation to live together without being married. The older generation had some difficulty adjusting. We would set off on our own into the countryside and often lost track of my grandmother's schedule. We'd sleep out on the warm sand of Capo di Feno's huge, deserted beach, amid the din of the breakers, around a little wood fire. Now and then we'd go to the family house in Ajaccio, where our carefree disregard for privacy ruffled a few feathers. My dear mother reprimanded us for giving my sisters—Valerie and Alexandra, the latter of whom was twelve years my junior—an indication of *la vie en rose* a little prematurely.

The Kiss Machine

YOU NOTICED HER height immediately, her marvellous bearing, the elegance of her walk and the beauty of her face, obviously, but perhaps even more so, its expression of joie de vivre, intelligence, and boundless vitality.

Her sky-blue eyes, emphasized by her black eyebrows and eyelashes, were always laughing. I gazed upon her constantly, moved by so much grace and love. She had a simplicity, a refinement. I often chose what she wore. I knew every inch of her soft skin; the down of her upper lip; the sweetness of her lower lip; the lobe of her flawless ear; the hollow where her neck and shoulder met, which was hardly ever covered up; her small, firm breasts, which loved to stiffen when they were caressed, especially the right one; her supple belly, which I often fell asleep on; her generous hips, which encouraged me in our lovemaking. Afterward, I'd move back up to her neck and drift off. We spent our life in big beds, naked, holding each other.

In the street, I'd take her by the elbow as if to say, *Hey, look everybody, this is my girlfriend!* We kissed and embraced shamelessly. Our families gave us an English nickname: Kiss Machine.

As twenty-year-olds, we used to worry about what our lovemaking would be like in the distant future, when we were forty. As forty-year-olds, even though she was ill, it was as sweet as ever. We read together, played music. We were inseparable. After my accident, she still played our lovers' games. We loved each other with our lips.

I always wanted to be close to her; in her presence, I felt handsome, more impressive.

*

OUR LIFE was set to music. Soon after we met in Reims, I rented a piano in a carpenter's cluttered storeroom, and she would come and meet me there. It was my Chopin-Schumann-Schubert phase. She would sit on a packing crate and listen while she read. At concerts we'd hold hands. One evening at a performance of Schubert lieder, thinking I was paying the beautiful singer an indecent amount of attention, she elbowed me hard in the ribs. When we moved to Champagne, she took singing lessons. Not a day would go by without us performing a Mozart duet or one of the other pieces we loved. Béatrice's mystery, who she was, was revealed by her singing. It came from deep within her, like a natural vibration. I always hoped we were in tune when we admired an especially beautiful passage, since rather than a song, I felt there was an almost sensual harmony in me. But I always took my cue from her breathing, from everything she did.

*

WHEREVER I was in the world, she was all that mattered to me: at night, pressed together, naked in our big bed, whispering about children, the certainty of being loved, the tenderness of our bodies. I have traveled constantly, yet the only real discoveries I have made on earth were in that big bed.

*

THE KING of Pinball transformed his image thanks to his stunning girlfriend. I settled my gambling debts by selling the beautiful orange Beetle I'd been given on my eighteenth birthday, and instead bought an old Citroën ID19 from the café owner, who had restored it beautifully. I took Béatrice everywhere in that rolling thunder. I was the king of the rapscallions and she was my queen.

One evening we were driving back to the university in Reims from Paris. It was slow going because of thick fog, but I didn't mind. Béatrice was pressed up against me, time didn't mean anything. I caught a glimpse of a sign saying we were coming into Meaux. It was impossible to see anything except the glare of the headlights reflected in the fog. I guessed where the train station was, figuring that every station has a hotel. Béatrice was surprised when I started ringing the bell and knocking on the door of the establishment in question, which seemed dead to the world. After a long while, a bad-tempered voice shouted at us to be quiet. I persisted. Finally the light came on. A black shawl in slippers led the way up the stairs. The floor creaked. Not a word until the door closed behind us. Béatrice was still pressed up against me. Still kissing, we got into the bed, which was lit by a forlorn bedside lamp. The wooden bed frame made an unbelievable racket. We laughed and whispered to each other all through that magical night, as the creaking echoed through the building. In the breakfast room the next morning, the shawl asked us if we'd slept well and Béatrice flushed up to her cheekbones. She bit into her hot croissant, not taking her eyes off me.

Sciences-Po students had to do an internship at the end of their second year. Béatrice and I had only just got engaged. My future father-in-law applied on our behalf to the Montpellier City Council and obtained a posting for us in its sister city of Louisville, Kentucky. We were both assigned to a small local bank: the Louisville Trust Company. Keen to please the prefect, the university arranged for us to stay with a local grande dame, an old woman who lived in a magnificent colonial mansion. Married several times, now widowed, she was thrilled at the arrival of the young couple. Carefully briefed, she greeted us with a curtsy worthy of a count and countess. She was so attentive that we couldn't get her out of our room. I had my suspicions that she spent some nights with her ear glued to the door, straining to hear the sighs that she lacked in her own life.

At the bank, Béatrice was assigned to the legal department while I poked my nose into estate management. We could take a fifteen-minute coffee break every two hours. We would rush off to the lift and spend the entire time kissing. This was shocking behavior from a puritan American point of view and confirmed the locals' image of the French. From then on, we were known exclusively as "the French lovers." We continued our antics in the street, provoking a range of excitable responses: screeching car brakes, honking horns, traffic jams, roars of laughter. One family of poor country folk stood rooted to the spot for five minutes staring until we were out of sight.

One evening our landlady rounded up all of Louisville's smart set for a barbecue around the swimming pool to introduce her aristocratic lovers. We were lovebirds without a cage—or inhibitions. As long as we were together, everything delighted us.

At night, we'd curl up, one behind the other, I'd put my hand on her hip and lift her hair off her neck, and then, on some subliminal signal, we'd swap positions in perfect synchronicity. We had our ways of making love, our games, our secrets, and at a given moment everything would arrange itself around this simple ballet. After the accident I could only lie on my back. She would rest her head in the crook of my neck, tell me where she was putting her legs, her arms, and then I'd try to imagine the position of her body.

It was agony not being able to caress her, not being able to make love to her.

She would snuggle in by my neck and my nights would revolve around the reality of my wife curled up against me. She never complained. She was tormented by the cancer that made her weaker every day; I was paralyzed and in constant burning pain. And yet we distilled, or rather expanded, our love to these two heads tenderly touching at night. Together we would escape.

Béatrice

WE'D BEEN EXPECTING our first child for four months when Béatrice started bleeding. I don't remember the hospital, I get them all mixed up these days, but I can still picture the young doctor. He was called Pariente, I know that for a fact. He told us with great kindness that we'd have nothing to worry about next time. I cried by Béatrice's bedside. Were my tears really because she had suffered? She was the one comforting me, after all. We were living in a high rise at Porte d'Orléans. Béatrice threw herself wholeheartedly back into student life.

The next time she became pregnant, the bleeding started in the third month. They gave me the fetus in a jar and asked me to take it to the laboratory. Why do I still remember that it was in the middle of the Bois de Boulogne? I can see myself entering the clinic. A woman in white greeted me. I put the flask on the counter. She seemed unsurprised. I left not knowing what to say, distraught.

They started to give us all sorts of tests. They sent me to have my sperm checked in a specialized lab. I hovered around indecisively until a nurse handed me an empty jar and pointed to a door. I went in, thinking I was going to see a doctor. Instead I found myself in a toilet full of pornographic magazines. After an eternity of shame, I handed back the container, the job done.

Our laboratory tests proved satisfactory.

We passed Sciences-Po with flying colors and decided to take the exams for the ENA.

Béatrice was twenty-five. She became pregnant again in March. Everything seemed fine. The prognoses were good. But then Béatrice had an embolism. She was determined to get through. The fetus didn't seem to have been affected. She wanted to have this baby at all costs, even that of her health. The chief resident spoke up for her harshly against a colleague who advocated using an anticoagulant, despite its risk of causing malformations. They were arguing in the corridor at the top of their voices. Béa was disgusted. How could two doctors forget that in room 21 there was a beautiful, intelligent, loving woman who, outside of that prison, was every bit their equal? When she could finally get up, she even saw she was taller than they were.

I spent the whole time there. The room was always full of flowers. There was fruit, books, music, a stocked refrigerator.

I had given up preparing for the ENA, forgotten the demands of the economy, the latest statistics, the daily world events. Our life—our *real* life, made of flesh and bone—was in here. We had to face it together. Thanks to credit transfers, I enrolled in a history degree. I regaled Béatrice with highlights from the lives of the first Arab navigators and the history of the Indian Ocean in the thirteenth and fourteenth centuries.

It's a handy system, credit transfers: we knew all about Ibn Battuta but not the succession of the French throne. I got my degree but we failed the child. After seven months' gestation, hypertension got the better of our child. We knew he was going to be a boy; he was starting to make his presence felt. Then he stopped moving.

The following month was a nightmare. The fetus had to decrease in size enough for Béa "to give birth naturally." The doctors prescribed long walks. I always went with her. She was exhausted, dazed. She didn't speak, wore her sunglasses permanently, avoided people. At night I rubbed her temples for hours. She'd cry herself into a stupor, or sometimes she'd let go and start shouting with hatred, rebelling.

She went into labor after dinner one night and we found ourselves in the emergency room. Béatrice told them the child was dead, but it made no difference: she would be treated the same as a woman who after several hours of pain would know happiness.

Then it was the moment of anguish, her womb was about to tear open. She looked at me. I looked at her encouragingly. She didn't want me to see. She asked for a sheet. Our heads were close but entirely separate. After she'd screamed for what seemed like a lifetime, her body relaxed. The dull throb of pain in her heart merged with that in her body. Her sunken eyes swam with tears.

Before we had time to recover, a drab character barged in without introduction and asked, "What was the name of the deceased?" Béa couldn't breathe. I rushed at the intruder, forced him out into the corridor. He explained that any child over seven months had to be registered, even if it wasn't alive at birth. I docilely answered all his absurd questions, signed all the documents until he was satisfied. I cried on my own in the corridor, then put on a brave face and went back to Béa. I talked to her calmly to try to comfort her and to hide my distress. Eventually she fell asleep. I stayed by her side, in a battered armchair. When she started sobbing, I'd put my hand on her forehead and whisper tenderly to her.

The following night, she had another embolism, another session in intensive care. I stayed with her. She was dizzy. Noises, light, vaguely audible conversations. A sleepless, grating night, morning never came. I held her hand throughout.

*

WE SET off for the United States to start a new life. We were recommended a good obstetrician, who meticulously prepared us for our fourth attempt. He was gentle, his clinic was luxurious, we were under the illusion that we had found a special haven, a place misery couldn't enter. To his surprise the pregnancy only lasted four months.

Under the strain of being left by our first American child, I was talking quietly to Béatrice one minute and the next . . . nothing. When I regained consciousness, the nurses teased me. Even Béa had a glint in her tired eyes.

Béatrice had two pulmonary embolisms. When they finally let her go after several months, she was a shadow of herself, only her eyes showed any signs of life. We went to Martinique. The minute we landed, we hired a boat, stocked up on supplies, and set sail.

Béatrice lying on a banquette; laughing at how hot a rain shower was; exclaiming with delight when the boat pitched too sharply; swimming for hours when we stopped in the middle of the sea; dancing naked the only time we saw another boat—this is what I remember about Béatrice, these moments of joyous self-assurance. In a few days she got her health and color back, and still had that sparkling glint in her eyes.

The learned American doctor convinced us he had worked it all out, that the only answer was to start again. We took him at his word. A year later, we lost another child, aged seven months.

We'd decided to adopt if it didn't work. We began the process: the letter of intent, the preadoption agreement, the go-ahead, all the different stages that might pave the way for an adoption . . . in five years. We wrote probably the most beautiful application Bogotá's Institute of Family Welfare had ever received. We went to a doctor for a checkup. He discovered an abnormality in Béatrice's blood test. He sent it by ambulance to the hospital in Cook County for further analysis. His diagnosis was confirmed. The condition had a barbaric name I still can't remember, but was commonly known as Vaquez's disease, a cancer of the bone marrow. It is generally found among the elderly, often men. As far as the chief resident knew, there were fewer than a hundred cases of women as young as Béatrice suffering from it in the United States. So now they'd got their guinea pig. From then on, the doctors in different hospitals would greet her with the same unfailing interest, the same comments about it being terminal for the old but that they were nevertheless able to prolong their lives by ten years or so. "So that's something," they would say. It was a cancer of the red blood cells. The hemoglobin developed so fast and intensely that the blood clotted. The most frequent cause of death was a pulmonary or cerebral embolism. You had to have chemo to destroy the red blood cells.

I was stunned. They'd said "cancer."

Béa was exhausted from her last miscarriage.

When they told me she had cancer, I lost my way. Everything went dark, as dark as the nights when I tried to escape with women, all women, any women.

Cherubino!

IN THE MIDST of all this insanity and pain, a telephone call informed us that a baby, a little girl, was waiting for us in Bogotá. Béatrice broke down, sobbing, in the middle of a packed French restaurant in Chicago. She had to go and be alone to get over the shock and to recompose herself.

I don't remember anything about those weeks, apart from the shame of how I ran away. Then the day came, in Bogotá, when Béatrice put Laetitia in my arms. She was a wonderful three-month-old baby, looking at me wide-eyed with surprise, and perhaps also anxiety. My breathing slowly matched itself to hers; all three of us began to breathe in sync. Béatrice leaned over my shoulder, looking down at the child, and there it was—we were off and running again. It had to happen. Laetitia was a miracle. Béatrice took pleasure in our lovemaking again. I rediscovered the warmth of her bruised body.

I had been made financial director of the French subsidiary of a big American pharmaceutical company. We were coming home, initially with trepidation, but now in triumph with our long-awaited child. Five years had passed since we'd left France. I moved them into the family town house. Béatrice was coming back to life; Laetitia was getting more and more beautiful. I worked relentlessly with my young boss, André, who became a friend. I earned half what I did in America but it was such an adventure! André would always bring a present for Laetitia when we worked at home on weekends.

*

BÉA WAS thirty-three. She was radiant.

Operation Heart

WE WERE DRIVING back from Saint-Gervais-les-Bains. Béatrice was tired and had stretched out full length in her seat. I heard her gasping and looked over. Hollow-eyed, she was finding it hard to breathe. Then it passed and she fell asleep. At every bend in the road, her head lolled from side to side.

I drove to Paris without stopping. When we got home, I woke Béa up. Her eyes still sunken, she stared at me blankly. She struggled up the stairs, then into bed. The night dragged on. I watched her as she slept fitfully. The next morning we decided to consult her cardiologist. He diagnosed a pulmonary embolism and had her hospitalized immediately.

A place was reserved for her in the coronary care unit. Our doctor's nephew was the chief resident. A stroke of luck. We didn't have time to go back home to kiss Laetitia. Saint-Antoine hospital . . . that was a new one to us.

As usual, we tried to joke. Each of us played our part.

Don't cry, not straightaway anyway. Good manners must out. We thanked the nurse. She was very nice. All of it was so familiar to us.

Our doctor's nephew appeared and got Béatrice settled in. She was a prisoner twice over—of her body and of the hospital regulations. They put her in uniform, a sort of white camisole worn without anything underneath. Everything was in place: drips, locks on the windows (to prevent suicides), no telephone, no TV, no color, restricted visiting times.

I wasn't having any of it. The medical team learned to compromise with my stubbornness. After a while, no one questioned my dogged presence anymore. The first night, when it was time for me to leave, I took the list of things you were allowed to bring in and reassured Béatrice: yes, I'd tell her parents and mine; yes, I'd kiss our little, two-and-a-half-year-old daughter.

The doctors ran tests and confirmed the pulmonary embolism. They put Béatrice in a permanently lit glass room and hooked her up to a cardiac monitor with a blinking red light and a line moving across a screen to indicate her heartbeat. Her food and drugs were administered by intravenous drip. She lay under the neon light, pallid and motionless, tears rolling down her face.

Béatrice had six pulmonary embolisms and spent a year in that hospital. I saw her every day but they were joyless visits. I didn't understand her loneliness. I didn't know what to say. I'd get there in the morning around eleven. My sight would be blurred, I'd be so anxious. She was happy to see me, even though I wouldn't say anything. By midday I had to get out, escape. I'd walk down rue Saint-Antoine.

I found an unspoiled, traditional neighborhood bistro. A couple owned it. The wife, a huge woman, did the cooking while the husband, gaunt from alcoholism, communicated solely with his elbows and shoulders, like a chicken. I always sat at the same table. The wife would make me a special first course and her delicious plat du jour. The heat would make me drowsy. I would fade out.

In the afternoon I would return to Béatrice under her neon lights. I would describe the street, the bistro, its smells, the menu. This would be our daily ritual for that entire year. She cried when her veins burst and they had to wrap her arms in alcohol-soaked bandages. Even though I was shattered, my presence seemed to please her, she still looked at me. Sometimes I stayed the night to reassure her. The one time she was able to go out after months in bed, she made herself up, disguising her sallowness as best she could, and struggled to my bistro. She was very girlish and vivacious, laughing about everything. When we left, she vomited on the sidewalk.

I worked unremittingly in the office, always putting in my ten hours, often staying late at night, weekends too.

But she expected more of me, in particular that I share her faith. I remained obstinately noncommittal on that score. Being near her was the only thing that kept my anguish at bay. Her attending physician, Dr. Slama, thought it was essential that she have a caval clip fitted, which would filter her blood to prevent clots from going up to her lungs. After weighing the risks of a fatal embolism against the slight possibility that the operation could have harmful consequences, we chose surgery.

They promised Béa the heart operation would only leave a little mark. In fact, she would never go swimming in a bikini again. The scar started in the middle of her sternum and ran down in a broad circle to just above her right buttock. She would have this huge, violet track for the rest of her life. I would be the only one who knew her secret.

When she finally emerged from the operating room, her eyes were closed. I took her hand. We'd won. . . .

So many years of suffering.

*

WHEN LAETITIA was four, we spent the summer holidays with cousins in Corsica on a huge sailing boat. The six chemotherapy tablets Béatrice had to take a day were our only reminder of her illness.

One day she was swimming breaststroke with our daughter. They were both laughing and splashing. She was radiant. When she scraped her ankle on a rock, she just gave a little scream and got back into the boat to clean the scratch. That wound would never heal. It was a side effect that they had concealed from us.

Béa's cancer thickened her blood, the chemo thinned it. The skin necrosed above her right ankle, forming an ulcer, and then did the same above the left one. The cancer should have been our biggest concern, and yet it was these horrible ulcers that traumatized Béa the most. She was hospitalized in Paris for six months a year, on average. Her parents were on duty constantly; I tried to fill in for them as much as I could. She always had a smile for me. I brought her tapes Laetitia had recorded for her; all our mail, which we forced ourselves to answer; and news from the outside world.

Her mother, a doctor, was disgusted by the various doctors' attempts to "treat" her ulcers. Complete butchery.

The pain made Béa weep.

*

THESE IMAGES come back to me yellow with nicotine. Smoke from all those hours spent chain-smoking seems to get into my eyes again. I remember how desolate and helpless I felt. But now that Béatrice is gone and my body is shattered, I forget the anger.

*

DR. FIESSINGER finally put an end to Béa's martyrdom. He prescribed home medical care and a traditional course of treatment, which involved scraping the wounds daily with a scalpel until the ulcers bled, a vital stage in cell reconstitution. I was in her bedroom for the morning and evening sessions, but I couldn't look at the scalpels. I would move my face close to hers and dry her tears.

How many times did she bite me hard enough to draw blood as they hacked her to pieces? And then, a few minutes later, it would all be forgotten. She was at home, with her family. This doctor had restored her to life. Now I had to protect her.

La Pitance

MOËT & CHANDON offered me a lucrative job in Champagne. We moved to La Pitance, a beautiful house backing onto Hautvillers Abbey, which the Benedictines had built in the seventh century. It was set in luxuriant parkland that rolled down to the Marne through the smoky air. The vines required constant tending, and, in the brilliant light, the shadows of their stakes looked like hundreds of sundials.

I was a member of the eleventh generation of the founding family. A representative of the twelfth, a baby we named Robert-Jean, joined our family around the time that we relocated to Champagne. When we went to get him in Bogotá, Laetitia came too. She was profoundly affected by the poverty of the children her age whom she saw begging on the streets, dressed in rags.

*

WE SPENT eleven years at La Pitance. Béatrice was its queen, Laetitia its princess, and Robert-Jean soon became its heir.

Despite Béatrice's illness and my exhausting work, those were happy years for the four of us. The seasons revolved around the fireplace; the piano; the garden; the cherry harvest; the hundreds of roses to prune; the jam making from different varieties of plums, apricots, and pears, which Laetitia liked to take a bite of while they were still on the branch.

I was made Pommery's managing director in Reims. Every morning, I'd drive Laetitia to school through the woods on a skiddy, winding, little road. The faster I went, the broader the smile on her face. We'd play a game: no braking on corners until the last minute, go over a hundred miles per hour on even a hint of straight road, always overtake dawdlers. She wouldn't let me drop her off in front of her school in my beautiful car; I'd have to leave her at the corner of the street so she could go and find her friends discreetly. Sometimes she'd come to my office and I'd introduce her to everybody, then she'd sit opposite me and "get on with some work." We were inseparable, which I think was difficult for Béatrice.

Our last party was for our daughter's thirteenth birthday. I put on a fireworks display that stunned Laetitia and her friends. None of the teenagers got a wink of sleep that night. Their shouts echoed through the vineyards.

Laetitia had already become a serious pianist by then. She had an exam to take. I wanted to be there. I should have been there. But I couldn't. I was detained on the big day by work commitments. And then I broke my neck.

Part Three

The Angel's Leap

Broken Wings

BÉATRICE WAS RECEIVING treatment at home, relieved to be back in her beautiful Pitance. I used to get up every morning at six thirty to go for a run. Leaving the house, I'd jog along the abbey wall and take the first lane that headed uphill, past an array of grimacing gargoyles. I'd study them out of the corner of my eye as Radowski, our dachshund, ran along, barking. A large, flat stretch on the right alongside the church, then another climb to get to the forest. My legs would already be aching by this stage. The path sloped back downhill to the left, so I'd pick up some speed. Radowski would already be two hundred yards ahead, and he would wait for me at the end of the lane. We'd come out onto the ridge separating the champagne vineyards from the forest. From here I'd have a bird's-eye view of the Marne winding through the valley, which would often be covered in fog. It felt as if we were on the roof of the world.

At first I ran a hundred yards, then gave up. But I went

farther every day. After a month I could run a two-mile lap through the forest and the vines without stopping. Soon running that twice wasn't enough, so one day, instead of turning back when I got to the end of the vines, I headed into the forest up a rough, slippery slope to the right. In a few months I could go straight up it without stopping. I was making light work of six miles a day; Radowski was following me now.

Later I had a friend who came with me. He was utterly tireless and would tell jokes, while I conserved my energies. We would run fifteen miles in a weekend, soon it was twenty. It felt as if I'd been reborn. Knee-high to a grasshopper, my seven-year-old son would trot along effortlessly at my side. Now I watch him set off, light-footed and resilient. He has inherited my urge to go the extra mile. I have run on every continent in the world.

After a while I was running thirty miles every weekend. Béatrice would be in bed, her legs covered in blood. I would pick up fresh bread on the way home and take her breakfast. She would prop herself up on her pillows and I would kiss her, dripping with sweat. She would be pleased: I was there for the first scalpel session of the day. Many years before, she had run in front of me on the shores of Lake Michigan in Chicago. I liked to hang back to watch her. Now and then I'd reach out and pinch her buttocks. She'd give a little scream and use it as an excuse to stop.

We spent one February with friends on an old farm in Chamonix. My friend Titi introduced us to his brother-in-law, who was encased in plaster from the neck down. He laughed as he told us about an accident he'd had paragliding. A friend had set off with his suspension lines knotted and banged himself on a rock face. Titi's brother-in-law had set off valiantly to help him, but ended up smashing into the mountain. His friend escaped with a few scratches.

He was amused by this "mishap," just as he was by an accident he'd had two months earlier while he was flying his small plane with his boss's daughter. The motor had fallen out, a loose bolt. He had managed to land in Lake Annecy and they'd swum to the bank. His sangfroid was the only reason they were still alive. A lovely, insane fellow. He got me started on paragliding by throwing me off a cliff.

It took me a few years and several survival courses to master paragliding but, in time, I was able to deflate my wing at thirty-two hundred feet, plummet through the air, and have the situation under control again with a few feet still between me and the water (as I would learn to my cost, it is a less dangerous business flying over water). Soon my flights grew longer. I'd land after five hours, exhausted. It was exhilarating to work out the position of a thermal by the rustle of leaves and to ride it, turning in constant circles until it let you go, your stomach in your boots, ten or twelve thousand feet above where you'd started. I came to love buzzards, which were another indication of the whereabouts of hot-air columns. Occasionally they'd dive-bomb toward me if I got too near their nests. Once I flew over Mont Blanc. It lay there, dazzling, at my feet. A huge eagle loomed overhead.

Soon I was crazy about paragliding. I would set off into the mountains with a backpack and stop wherever I felt the beauty of a place calling to me. At first I went so far as to wear a cap and a tie, but that stopped when I lost too many caps and ruined too many ties to mention. I soon had hundreds of flights behind me.

A typical flight would begin with me cavalierly unrolling my canopy and studying the ground, as everyone else bustled about. I'd measure the gaps between the bubbles of hot air flattening the grass, work out when the next one was coming, and arch my back to position the canopy directly over it. There . . . perfect. While the other amateurs launched themselves into space, pitching and rolling like a ship in high seas, I'd simply apply a little break and ascend in my chosen thermal like a helicopter taking off. I'd thrust my upper body forward to steer, and let out a cry; I was an eagle. If the right tip of the wing lifted up with a shudder, I'd rock my body with my left leg crossed over my right, left hand slightly forward, right hand back a fraction. I'd turn into the core of the thermal repeatedly until it ejected me, usually at the base of a cloud. I knew it wasn't allowed, but I still loved going up as far as I could. No one would follow me that high. I'd emerge from my cloud, then set off on another thermal. I'd stretch out my legs and tip my head back for the best glide ratio, then light a cigarette. Sometimes I'd even roll one. I'd adjust my Walkman headphones. How many times did I fly singing Bellini's *Norma* at the top of my lungs!

I flew endlessly, thousands of feet above the other wings,

above the mountains, and, on one memorable occasion, above two Mirage jets. Another time a glider crossed in front of me with a dizzying, hissing noise. At times I was afraid. Once I even found myself over Switzerland without a passport. I would nibble on a bar of chocolate and drink from the pipette fixed to the side of my helmet, and I'd never want to come down. Then, just as I was thinking I'd lost everyone, the radio would call my name. They would have spotted my wing from the ground a few thousand feet below. Time to go back. I'd wrap the break line three times around my right hand, jam it under the harness, and shift my weight in the same direction. The wing's leading edge would start dropping faster and faster into the turn. Soon it would be vertical and I'd be horizontal, spinning around. We'd dive in a hellish ballet, the wing and I, falling three, six, nine thousand feet, under control but at dizzying speed. Then I would raise my hand a few hundred feet above the landing area. I'd stand up in the harness, grab all the suspension lines except the two in the middle, sit back down, and fold in the flapping wing tips so that only the center would remain inflated. I would sink toward the landing point. Seven feet from the ground, I would release the lines and apply the brakes; the wing would reinflate with a few inches still to go and set me down like a butterfly alighting on a flower.

The heavens were my element. I was like an angel.

Then one day I crashed into something that was either the green grass or hell.

Crash Landing

I WAS LYING ON the mountainside, just feeling a little numb. I must have passed out. Max and Yves, my paragliding friends, had put their wings down next to mine. Max, who was a doctor, had taken over. He'd dug a hole by my face so I could breathe and was on the radio to base. I didn't know why they wouldn't touch me. I was talking to them, my breathing was calm. So why did they keep asking me if I could breathe? A stalk of grass tickled my nose, I sneezed, then started laughing. Max was going ballistic on the radio. He was demanding they send a helicopter from Grenoble, not Chambéry; Chambéry was closer though. Yves was talking to me like a child and he looked as if he were shaking. I didn't seem to be able to move.

I lapsed back into unconsciousness, then was woken by a tremendous noise. It was the helicopter trying to hold steady in strong winds. A doctor and a fireman jumped out, then it lifted up and hovered overhead. I couldn't feel anything. They carefully moved me on my back onto a stretcher. I saw the sky and the helicopter above me. They were going to take me with them. My friends and the others were going to stay behind. I called to Yves, I'd realized there was a problem. I asked him to telephone Béatrice immediately, to tell her that it wasn't serious, that I loved her, that she had always been the one, that she was the light of my life. "Call my parents, tell them to be kind to her, not to let her go through it on her own." They had been complaining about my paragliding for ten years; once they'd even said they wouldn't look after the children if I had an accident. Béatrice had started crying. I should have said something, but they were right. I was in tears talking to Yves. I wanted him to tell my parents they had to take care of my family. Yves calmed me down. I gave him my secretary's telephone number so she could cancel my meetings that evening in Italy, the following day in Switzerland, and the day after that in Germany.

The helicopter lowered a cable. Before I was winched up, I apologized to Yves for spoiling his day. I swayed about in the air. The copilot leaned down to grab me and hauled me aboard. It was impossible to hear anything in the cabin after that. They put an oxygen mask on me.

We landed on the roof of the hospital in Grenoble. I was raced into the anesthetizing room. Faces bent down to me and we talked. A man, it must have been the surgeon, interrupted our pleasantries, saying "There's more. It's urgent." Those were the last words I heard for a long time.

I later learned how difficult the operation was. Béatrice and my parents managed to get to the hospital in a few hours. They were met by the surgeon saying, "He's got a twenty percent chance of pulling through."

After the operation, my body refused to breathe. They put me in an artificial coma for a month so that the ventilator could do its work without being rejected by my body.

Béatrice spent the entire month at my bedside, talking to me, telling me stories—to the intense irritation of the surgeons, who thought it was all a waste of time. Béatrice didn't let up for a moment in her campaign to get me out of there. She called Fred Chandon, my main boss, and André Garcia, my ex-boss and friend. They got me admitted to La Pitié-Salpêtrière Hospital in Paris. I stayed there for more than two months.

I was in a coma for a few days after I arrived, then Dr. Viars opted for a sort of medical interlude. This involved abruptly taking me off all the medicine I'd been on, including the twenty-four capsules of Imovane that were keeping me in the coma. It was a massive shock. For a week, I had a fever of between one hundred and four and one hundred and six degrees. I contracted hepatitis, but gradually I returned to something approximating consciousness. I came back to earth under Béatrice's watchful gaze. I don't remember what she said, only the look in her eyes.

For the next few weeks, I was adrift in an imaginary world. Béatrice managed the constant procession of relatives, all of

whom ended up in the nightmares possessing me. My visions
were so real, they sucked everything into their narratives.

*

*I am on a small motorboat, coming into shore. I row
the last stretch and tie up on the other side of my hospital room. Then there's a deafening noise and I'm being
moved to the cabin of a Mirage jet flown by a Spanish pilot. I find out later that social services has hired a
Spaniard to cut costs. The pilot's job is to pick up enough
speed in a nosedive to take me through the sound bar-
rier. It has to be outside French territory. Every day I get
into his plane. I return shaken up but rested. Finally the
plane drops me in Egypt, east of Alexandria.*

*The hospital orderly takes me on a tour of the city's
suburbs. He sets me down in a café, which looks like a
medieval tavern. It is a large wood-paneled room arranged like a shopping mall with several floors. There
are crowds of people. Some are eating Chinese food or
taking Turkish baths. Others, like me, are lying in a
confined space. Someone passes us a water pipe.*

*The orderly takes me into the white-tiled bathroom.
Jets of steam shoot over my head. I try to prop myself
up on my elbows but I can feel myself slipping down
toward the drain in the middle of the room. The orderly
has just abandoned me. I shout to stop myself from being
sucked in, but it's no use.*

*

MIRAGES, DELUSIONS. When I opened my eyes, I didn't have a body anymore.

*

My little sister Alexandra is here. Something is terrifying her—she splutters when she tries to speak, she is sheet white. She's about to leave when her boyfriend Leo and a gang of drug addicts storm in. They stab the nurse to death, throw themselves on the medicine cabinet, and make off with syringes and pharmaceuticals. There's a screech of nails and everyone disappears. I must have dreamed it. But I hear on the radio the next day that the police have surrounded a dangerous group of thugs who are dancing and shouting around a young woman with a knife stuck in her back. They can't get close to the victim. It's Alexandra. I cry out.

*

COUSIN NOUNS had come to see me, as he would every day of my incarceration. He told me his usual hilarious stories, which made me split my sides laughing. He was followed by my twin brother, Alain. Clicking his heels together, he bent forward from the torso over my bed, gave a military salute, and said "Chin up, bro . . . th . . . ther!" He straightened up slightly, then reverted to his customary mute state, standing unwaveringly at attention. Finally Béatrice appeared. "Dismiss!" The warmth in her eyes let me know I was alive. She reached out and touched me. She was the only one who bent down to kiss me wherever she could.

*

I'm with Emmanuel, my son's godfather and a graduate of the École Polytechnique, and Marie, his delightful Chinese wife, in the garden in Champagne. It is getting dark, we're starting to shiver, when suddenly a mass of Chinese children comes out of Marie's ears. Marie rounds them up. Emmanuel gives me a little, embarrassed smile. He explains he did something wrong on his computer. Now computers have triggered a world war. Rapacious microchips are escaping from the screens like fleas and attacking enemy machines. Emmanuel tells us the latest news from the front. It turns out it's the Tibetans with their low salaries who have started hostilities from their high mountains. We—Emmanuel, Marie, her horde, and I—decide to go to Tibet. Everything started when a simple young man set up a small company with his wife and mother to make computer chips using a revolutionary process. The Chinese army took them prisoner and now the wretches work night and day to supply their jailers. After incredible adventures, we escape from Tibet and move to New York.

The war seems to be running out of steam because

of a shortage of chips, when A. B. storms into our offices with a pack of gorillas. He is extremely gentle. He is interested in Emmanuel's work and that of a Tibetan who has become our friend. Behind A. B., a wizened old woman with a thick Spanish accent is yelling terrible things. A. B. wants a majority share of our company. We refuse politely. They slit the old woman's throat. Our Tibetan friend, whose name escapes me, vanishes with a compassionate smile after committing the Tibetan form of hara-kiri. The survivors are taken prisoner. War breaks out again.

I am in a cage hanging from the bedroom ceiling of A. B.'s mistress, Isabelle Diange. She is surrounded by young drug addicts; they have orgies while a protégé of A. B.'s plays bewitching music. From time to time, my cage is lowered down to de Diange's bed by pulleys, where she's waiting for me, limbs flamboyantly akimbo. I penetrate her from the cage. God, how could I? Sometimes they throw me peanuts. She loves someone else, an unrivaled singer. A. B. is furious, but, most of all, he's ruined.

Suddenly there's a massive explosion, followed by an oppressive silence. The floor is littered with corpses. They're blue, with no obvious wounds, apart from the monstrous grimaces on their faces. They've died of cold. I find Béatrice and the children and we set off by train to find warmth. A. B. is sitting opposite us. He's wearing a thick fur, his skin hardly looks cold. The country we travel through is barren and frozen.

The dead are thrown out of the windows. Soon Béatrice can't keep warm anymore—the rings under her eyes and her lips have turned purple. I pull the alarm cord and carry her out onto the hard snow. The children follow in single file. I find a mud hut surrounded by a huge pile of logs. We sit around the fire for a few years. Despite the persistent cold, the weather improves. One day our son, whose voice has broken, sees a little white flower out the window. A snowdrop. We have to wait three more years for the ground to be covered in yellow daffodils, Béatrice's favorite color. Then we go back to Paris.

*

NOTHING HAD changed. I was back in my hospital bed. One day I thought I saw Reynier come into my room, crying. Was he crying over me, over himself, or over all these terrible things that were happening? I never knew—he didn't come back.

*

The details of the accident come back to me.

Who's this man kidnapping Béa and taking her off to a chalet?

My cousin Catherine introduces me to a couple of researchers. They're both thin and they seem profoundly sad. They have developed a complex electronic system designed to reconstitute bone marrow cells. They have only brought the part that can regenerate heels and feet.

I want to try it immediately. They fit a white plastic mold to my left heel. It has a mass of wires coming out of it, which they briskly connect to a box that looks like a battery charger. When everything is ready, they wait for me to give them the signal. I've got nothing to lose. "Go!" I say.

I don't feel anything at first, then a slight tingling. It grows more intense, starts stinging, then it becomes something much worse, a searing feeling. Just as I smell burning flesh, they disconnect the wires. They put the mold back in its box. The young woman massages my heel with a greenish ointment. Neither says a word. My cousin Catherine looks stunned. One of my toes twitches. After a minute, I can bend all five toes and rotate my foot around the ankle.

It's a miracle!

"Why doesn't anybody know about your technique?"

"We're at the experimental phase," says the young woman researcher. "We haven't completed the full prototype for quadriplegics yet, but we are meant to present it to the hospital board in Paris in six to eight weeks."

*

TIME PASSED. I told Béatrice I was worried that I hadn't heard from the researchers. Drawing on all her reserves of patience, she worked out that I was saying I'd met two people through Catherine. She came back the next day and told me Catherine didn't know whom I was talking about.

I blushed like I used to as a child when I was caught lying. I couldn't breathe. Béatrice tried to comfort me by saying she'd talk it over with Catherine.

*

That evening, the nurse explains they've changed my treatment and upped my dose of Prozac.

The next morning I have trouble waking up, I feel numb all over. Even my left foot doesn't react anymore.

*

BÉATRICE TRIED to awaken my interest by telling me stories about the family, reading the newspapers, switching on the hospital television, but nothing worked.

*

I am jolted out of my lethargy one evening by the sight of the two researchers engaged in an impassioned debate on TV. I don't understand what they're saying immediately. The program doesn't seem live, somehow—it's as if normal programming had been overridden by a video. The researchers look thinner than ever. They are protesting strongly against the board of management for Paris's hospitals, which is denying them the right to speak. I try to get a copy of the video from the matron. She pretends not to understand. I didn't dream it, though. The orderly bears me out. He has just seen them on TV himself.

That evening, my doses are increased again. My periods of lucidity become fewer and farther between.

The researchers can heal us, all of us who lie here breathing through our trach tubes, groaning. All these people who have to spend months in the hospital will be free again.

One night I have trouble breathing. The oxygen from the ventilator isn't getting through the trach. Pressing the buzzer with my head, I ring for the nurse. No one comes. I keep ringing. It's no use. I'm going to suffocate.

I must have blacked out. When I open my eyes dawn is breaking—the shift changes in an hour. I just have to hold out until the orderly comes. When he comes into the room, he rushes toward me, realizes what's happening immediately, and restores the flow of oxygen.

I sleep all day. That night, they put a young woman with black hair in the bed next to me. She is screaming in agony. It looks as if she hasn't got any legs. They give her injections that quiet her down. A light goes out at the other end of the ward, then another. The first one is relit. All the lights around me keep coming on and going out. The game stops when my light goes out.

I look down to check. The ventilator is still working.

It must be plugged into a separate socket. But the young woman with black hair and two other patients are dead. None of this can go any farther than this hospital wing. I can't shake off the feeling that I am the target of a conspiracy. I feel guilty every time the medical team goes silent in my presence. It feels that, unintentionally, I'm a threat to them. They've got rid of the researchers, so now I'm the only witness to what they're up to.

*

I USED the computer my friend had set up for me to compose a message to Béa. Two hours later, exhausted, I'd finished an SOS. I fell asleep. I was surprised to wake up after a very peaceful night's sleep. Béa arrived. I indicated she should take the floppy disc and read it outside the hospital—she could be caught otherwise. The day passed. I began to wonder whether I had any reason to worry. I dozed off.

*

A deafening racket wakes me up after dinner. I can hear pounding feet, shouts, orders, furniture being shunted around—even machine-gun fire, I think. My door is violently thrown open, a squad bursts into my room and takes up position around my bed. They're all wearing riot gear. They're all at least sixty years old.

My father-in-law comes in last. As a former prefect, he has been able to make arrangements quickly to protect me and to call in colleagues from the national police.

*

BÉATRICE WAS there. She was telling me about the children.

*

My father-in-law positions his men in the corridor and in my room. Fighting breaks out. His men stand firm. Thinking it will be safer, they move me to the top of an oak tree in the garden and put me in a hammock. Snipers posted on the hospital roof kill one of my guards before a grenade gets them. Groups of journalists have been arriving for a while, and now they've surrounded the battleground. Talking into a microphone, I explain what's happening and call on the prime minister to mediate. He arrives with a huge entourage and orders everyone to stop fighting. I demand that the researchers be given a chance to operate on me. An international appeal goes out. A few days later, the young female researcher appears, unrecognizable in dark glasses and dyed hair. She is hoisted up the oak tree with her equipment. She is weak. Skirmishes break out again when she checks a plug that has been reserved for her in the hospital. Trembling all over, she finishes connecting the wires after dark. Flares light up the scene. Before she turns on the machine, I kiss my father-in-law, thank him, and ask him to look after Béatrice and the children.

*The young woman pulls the lever and I close my
eyes. . . . Nothing. Nothing happens. Then suddenly,
there's a blinding ball of sparks. I faint.*

*

I WAS in my hospital bed, motionless. Béatrice was there, talking to me about the children. I sobbed so hard I started chok-
ing. Béatrice asked if I was in pain. "I haven't got an answer
to your message, I'm afraid," she said. "I did something wrong
on the computer and wiped everything off the floppy."

Everything fell to pieces at that point. I lapsed into complete silence. Finally, one night, consumed by guilt, unable
to accept my condition, terrified by the madness taking me
over, I decided to kill myself. But it's hard for a quadriplegic to commit suicide. I managed to wrap the oxygen tube
around my neck, jerk my head back, and lose consciousness.
I was woken up by a bright light. The nurses, alerted by the
machine's alarm, reconnected me as if nothing had happened.
Then the real silence began.

Kerpape

I HAD BEEN ON my back for more than a year. Béatrice had devoted every last ounce of her strength to me. We were so close, I felt we'd become one person. With our battered bodies, we were the darlings of Kerpape, the rehabilitation center on the Brittany coast. She was so beautiful, I felt I was walking on water in that world of shipwrecked humanity. The sea at our feet lulled us to sleep, soothed our dreams. Béatrice's blood count was stable, the range was normal; the doctors couldn't explain it. She came with me everywhere, encouraged me in all my exercises. Our days were non-stop.

It took me months to learn to sit up. In Kerpape, they lay you on a tilt table in a room with large windows looking out onto the Atlantic. Every day they increase the slope by a degree until the triumphant moment when you find yourself upright, strapped to this table, finally able to look the physios and nursing auxiliaries in the eye. No more looking up nostrils! And then you can sit in a wheelchair.

I was virtually horizontal in mine, with the controls under my chin. But in no time I was an ace driver and having races with the children of the center, who were a fearless bunch. They may have been suffering horrifically, those youngsters, but they laughed and were lighthearted, and grown-ups found their hilarity contagious. It was impossible not to be affected by the spirit of hope that reigned in the center. Every patient was a unique case. At the bottom of the hierarchy were "the knees," the people who'd walk again one day. They were always ready to help the quadriplegics, who were understood by all to be at the top. Then there were the people in plaster towers with metallic frames rising above their heads. They were so fragile they had to be set in concrete. One of them, an African guy, laughed so hard once that he slowly tipped over backward. No one could stop him. His whole body fell on the floor. We heard a crash of plaster and metal hitting the ground. He survived though.

Béatrice had a kind word for everyone, and she sometimes spent time with people if they were feeling down. It was obvious to us when someone was depressed: they wouldn't come to the cafeteria, preferring to cry on their own in their rooms; then she'd see if she could visit them. The nursing staff showed degrees of kindness and gentleness that seemed inconceivable in a hospital environment. Patients stayed for a long time, a year on average. A young man named Christophe had been there for five. He had caught a virus as a child and now he was a quad like me. He was cold all day long and wouldn't budge from the wall radiators. Even in summer, when the sun blazed through the windowpanes, you'd find him at one, sweating but frozen. Quads have a problem with their thermostats: their body temperature isn't regulated in a normal way. Despite the neuropathic burning scalding me on the outside, my bones were often cold. I felt like a frozen steak that had been dipped in the pan and was being eaten while the middle was still crispy with ice. A lot of people smoke to warm themselves up; if they have had a tracheotomy, they smoke through the gaping hole in their throat. How many shirts, pants, and blankets have I burned through without being able to feel a thing until, finally—the smell of smells—I've caught a whiff of grilling flesh?

We gave a nickname to every nurse: Jaja de Mon Cœur, Dis-Moi Madie, Cri-Cri, Do, Marie-Laine, Jo. Not to mention Annick aux Baisers Fougueux, Brigitte Candide, Yo-Yo Parfumée, Béatitude, Sophie la Rousse, Françoise Ma Sœur, Louis le Druide, Jojo le Papa, Joël le Quintal, Jean-Paul le Toubib, and Busnel le Big-Boss.

Angels, every one of them.

QUADS LOSE the use of their chest muscles. They breathe with difficulty from their diaphragms. It took me months to master the reflexes you need for this type of breathing. Some never manage. They remain permanently connected to a ventilator.

The water in the swimming pool was around ninety

degrees so we wouldn't get cold. I felt like an astronaut in zero gravity. Nothing restrained me physically. I could have turned upside down without being able to do anything about it. Two rings under my arms supported me, another around my neck. My pains seemed to ease. I floated, the water caressed my face. The sound of children echoed around as I sunk into a sweet torpor.

The strong personalities became apparent during meals in the cafeteria, when funny stories would be relayed from one end of the room to the other. Every day some food would go down the wrong way and a patient would fill his or her lungs rather than stomach. This could be fatal. The caregivers would rush over, the whole room would wait in silence. When normality was restored, the laughter would start up again, louder than ever. They were all aware of their fragility. Each respected the other's suffering. There was a genuine sense of fellowship between us. Twice my wheelchair shot off on its own accord without my being able to control it. I bulldozed the whole table into the wall. There were shouts of alarm but no one was hurt.

Our children had started at the nearby school in Larmor-Plage. They became a part of the big Kerpape family.

IT WAS so sad for all the young people who now found themselves alone, most of whom had been in love and sometimes engaged or even recently married. Mainly it was men who left their broken women. But women sometimes cracked up too. Love affairs started between wheelchairs. There was a tall, very hunched young woman who had been left by her fiancé. I think half the center was in love with her. She was infinitely sad.

We never lingered on the traumatic brain injury floor. I once saw a family with four young children walk past in silence. Suddenly the husband started screaming and thrashing around—he had had a total personality change. The mother was crying, the children were clinging to her. He had to be taken away. Traumatic brain injury is hell. Without appearing to have changed on the outside, those affected can become entirely different people on the inside.

In the hospital, I discovered the misery of pain, the loneliness of the crippled, the way the old and unproductive can be excluded, the loss of innocence endured by so many young people. I was entirely sheltered from this suffering until the accident gave me a glimpse of its enormity. Some young people spend a year in those centers. They don't have television or radio or visitors. They hide away and cry, anguished and guilt-ridden and gripped by a sense of extreme injustice.

Cyril, one of our fellow patients, was suffering from a progressive illness, which they hadn't been able to identify. He was slowly dying in his tiny wheelchair. Then one evening he put on a show. It was an exclusive audience, just us patients, with Cyril up on stage. His skits made us cry with laughter. Moving jerkily because of his chronic fatigue, he performed a striptease that involved not only taking off all his clothes but also stripping his chair of all accessories, even the wheels, because you couldn't get those on welfare.

We laughed with Cyril and the others until the early hours. Béatrice was curled up against me in my little bed. She fell asleep on my shoulder. We had never felt so at peace. The children were being looked after by friends.

We would have suffered less if we'd never woken up.

*

BÉATRICE WAS exhausted. She hadn't left my side for sixteen months. Her illness seemed to have run its course. It was a trap though. The more energy she invested in me, the higher the price she'd have to pay when the time came.

I was happy in Kerpape. Béatrice was friends with everyone. Our children divided up the patients amongst themselves, each taking responsibility for half. I kept up with work, made decisions. I felt in control. Béatrice was due a rest. She needed a change of scene, to get her bearings. She didn't want to leave me, but I insisted. Finally, she allowed herself three weeks in Corsica.

It was a complete disaster, for her and for me. I hadn't mourned the loss of my body; her presence was the only thing keeping me going. Suffocating depression set in immediately. I buried myself away in my bed. I lost the power of speech.

The shrinks tried to help me ascribe a meaning to the accident. Had I been afraid of Béatrice dying? Was I sacrificing myself in place of the hundreds of people that Pommery, for the first time in fifty years, wanted to lay off? I'd always been drawn to extremes. Was this just one rush of speed too many? Did I want to be closer to Béatrice, to share her suffering, feel her anxieties? Maybe . . .

WITH HER away, it was as if I didn't exist anymore. I had no will, no desire. Habit alone kept me levitating on the flotation mattress. I wanted to sleep but I couldn't. I was tormented by thoughts. I had tried to support her, make her feel better, but I had run away too, terrified. How could I have been such a coward? I wanted to disappear.

Her anguish showed through the letters she sent me every day. She was afraid she wouldn't be able to cope. The children were acting up. She felt terribly alone in the Corsican mountains—there was no gentleness there anymore. Kissing, hugging, the tenderness of a hand, a child's head on your shoulder—would we ever experience any of that again? I was afraid for her, alone and exhausted. Would we ever get our confidence back?

We had never envisaged disaster.

A New Partner in the Firm

AFTER A YEAR of rehabilitation in Brittany, we gave up
La Pitance. Béatrice moved us into a beautiful ground-floor
apartment in the middle of Paris. She did all the work to it,
adapted it for me. My father-in-law applied to the Defence
Health Service, with the result that Jean-François, a young
legionnaire wounded in the Gulf War, was assigned to help
with my transport. He was a taciturn fellow who lived with a
wolfhound. Everything was fine for three months until Béatrice was hospitalized again. I asked Jean-François to pick me
up from the hospital at eight one evening. By eleven he still
hadn't arrived. Finally he showed up and bundled me into
his converted van without saying a word. The trip back was
like a scene out of an action flick. He didn't stop at a single
red light. My chair skidded from one side of the stock car to
the other. Suddenly he jammed on the hand break at a green

light leaving the van slewed across the road, and, still without saying anything, jumped out. He beat up two people in the car behind us who had supposedly been trying to overtake him as he zigzagged along. Then he got behind the wheel again in catatonic silence to see me back home. I was furious and helpless; I waited until he had got me to bed before telling him his services would no longer be needed. He explained in a dignified way that he had started drinking again. We parted company on good terms.

Abdel was the first to answer the job announcement. There were ninety applicants in all, only one of whom was French. By a process of elimination, I ended up with Abdel and the Frenchman, and decided to give each of them a trial week. I felt that Abdel was his own person, was good at reading situations, and had a caring—almost maternal—streak. What's more, he was a good cook, even if he did leave the kitchen a mess.

The Frenchman was unfortunate enough to have told me that bringing a Muslim into your home was like letting in the devil. That was a mistake, since I hired Abdel the same day. We had converted a 215-square-foot studio apartment for him on the top floor. He had room, board, laundry, and a good salary. It was the first time in his life, he admitted to me one day, that he had been treated with respect. He'd only ever done odd jobs and been paid peanuts before. As his pride knew no bounds—something that I was to find out later—he had also on occasion walked out on employers on his first day, after hitting them to teach them good manners if necessary.

He told me once about the trauma he'd suffered as a child, and I saw tears of frustration on his face. His parents had more than ten children. When he was three they gave him to his paternal uncle, who was childless. It was, apparently, a common practice in Algeria at the time, but he could never accept this. Usually a fierce loner, he felt welcomed into our family.

He bore the whole world a grudge. He was only five feet six and to compensate he had become unusually strong. He'd lay into anyone who "disrespected" him, man or woman.

"It's wrong to hit a woman," I'd tell him.

"She shouldn't have called me a dirty Arab then."

Naturally, he wouldn't mention the fact that he'd accelerated while the woman was still on a pedestrian crossing or cut her off or that she hadn't responded to his pick-up line or whatever it might be.

Some women refused his advances, but I was amazed at how many did not. I even saw some write their telephone numbers on the palm of their hand while their husbands were there—something that didn't seem to deter Abdel's interest. Another woman accepted his overtures while she was with her mother and her daughter.

It has to be said that he was hilarious and had an innocent cheekiness, which must have aroused their protective instincts, even if he did look like a little devil.

One afternoon a woman rang up, screaming and sobbing. I calmed her down, then asked her to tell me what was wrong.

I couldn't believe my ears. She had met Abdel for the first time that afternoon. She had asked him to take her out to dinner. "No problem," he had replied, which was surprising, given that Abdel refused to put himself to any expense for his conquests.

He had then "happened" to pull over by Père Lachaise Cemetery and, seeing as they were there, had asked her for an "aperitif." The young woman, who can't have been a complete novice, described in every conceivable detail the exercise that she had had to perform to satisfy our friend's pressing need. Once it had been met, he had asked her to get something out of the trunk of the car. . . . Then he had screeched off and abandoned her. I promised his date I would give Abdel a stern talking-to.

Abdel came home. I told him disapprovingly what I'd just heard. It took him ten minutes to recover from his hysterics. He concluded that he had saved himself the price of a meal and an actual aperitif. He told me a handful of similar stories until I stopped him, disgusted.

There was only one woman who terrified him: my darling daughter Laetitia. If I wanted to see her, I had to ring her in her room myself so that Abdel wouldn't have to knock on her door. Never, he told me, had a girl treated him so briskly. It did him a great deal of good.

His relations with men, meanwhile, boiled down to the principle of "Might is right." In a tough world, he thought, you had better be the toughest of them all.

One afternoon Abdel parked by our building, blocking a neighbor's parking space, and went back to the apartment to lock up. I was in the car; Laetitia was in the front passenger seat. Next thing we knew a car with diplomatic license plates had pulled up—the neighbor—and started honking vehemently. This didn't make Abdel move any faster. In fact he came around to check that I was strapped in properly. The driver pounded on his horn, his face scarlet. Abdel ambled around to his door. Exasperated, the neighbor stormed out of his pretty Volvo and insulted him. He was American, a head taller, and sixty pounds heavier than Abdel. Still, Abdel grabbed him by the collar: "What's your problem?" The fellow objected in broken French to his scruffiness and lack of manners. First head butt. The American's gums started bleeding. He was livid, demanding to see his attacker's employer. Slightly paler than usual, Abdel pointed me out in the back of the car, then punched him hard twice for good measure. I flinched in my chair. Laetitia was so embarrassed that she had laid herself flat across the front seat. The American was thrown, though. He retreated to his car, apologizing, then backed up to let us pass. Abdel laughed for a good five minutes; the altercation had been a tonic. I used to think he only relaxed after doling out the day's quota of punches.

He was surprised if I lectured him about his behavior. When I gave preparatory school classes on ethics and management, he generally fell asleep after five minutes. When I talked about hope in schools or churches, he'd catnap standing up.

He had attended school for as short a time as possible—just long enough to hit some of his teachers and witness the gang rape of another, in which, he assured me, he hadn't taken part.

He spent all his youth in a housing project on the outskirts of Paris, where learning to steal and deal drugs were essential survival skills. He'd laugh when he talked about French prisons, those "proper hotels." According to him, plenty of people in the projects spent their winters in jail to be nice and warm before coming out in summer to engage in their nefarious activities.

He respected me, I sensed, because I thought he was intelligent and deserved something other than a wretched future. My family's privileged background seemed completely alien to him, given that he was only familiar with the rough world of the streets. Nevertheless he brought up my son with great kindness and Robert-Jean treated him like an older brother.

Abdel never slept for more than a few minutes at a time, but he could do so in any position. His driving was as extravagant as every other aspect of his life, and it was not unusual for him to fall asleep behind the wheel. This made me nervous. It was my job to keep him awake. I tried, but he still caused endless accidents, including one that occurred when I was lying on the pressure sore mattress in the back of the stock car. We had already been on the highway for three hours when there was a huge crash. I was catapulted forward between the passenger seat and the door. My face was covered in blood; I couldn't speak. The fire brigade arrived and attended to the other passengers. Finally one of the firemen opened the back door and then shut it immediately, shouting "Dead body!" Abdel disentangled me, straightened the bumper with a metal bar, and eventually set off, pretending nothing was wrong and shouting about some woman who he said had cut him off. In fact, he had fallen asleep. He was so proud though, he never admitted it. "I'm the best," he'd say constantly, then laugh. He believed it implicitly, so wouldn't listen to a word of criticism.

He was unbearable, vain, proud, brutal, inconsistent, human. Without him, I would have rotted to death. Abdel looked after me without fail, as if I was a babe in arms. Attentive to the smallest detail, close to me when I was miles away from myself, he set me free when I was a prisoner, protected me when I was weak, made me laugh when I cried. He was my guardian devil.

Part Four

A Second Wind

Witnesses

WHEN BÉATRICE FIRST brought the children to see me after I'd been in intensive care for three months, I couldn't talk because of the tracheotomy. Laetitia went to incredible lengths to make sure I'd seen her. She played a little game, sneaking behind the other family members who were leaning over my bed and giving them donkey's ears, pulling funny faces behind their backs. I watched her antics, thinking she was wonderful. And she saw the laughter in my eyes that my mouth full of tubes couldn't give her.

Of course I was full of remorse, that useless feeling that eats away at you forever. If only I could have avoided the events of June 23, I wouldn't have worn Béatrice to the bone, tormented Laetitia, left Robert-Jean so vulnerable. Oh, the effort they put in to keep me going. It was too much to ask of them, they were too young. The present began that day for me.

*

I WAS on an air-fluidized bed for six weeks, experiencing the sensation of floating as warm air circulated the microscopic beads that kept me in a state of levitation. The heat, the purr of the blower, the lack of any temporal cues gradually loosened my hold on reality. I receded into the distance; my brain turned to mush. All this just to heal my ass!

Bedsores are a bane of paralysis. An object—a piece of furniture, say—only has to be in contact with our bodies for fifteen minutes (we don't feel anything) for our flesh to split open. It then needs months of care for it to heal up.

On a number of occasions I have been treated to the delights of bedsores on my heels, my elbows, my knees, and my sacrum—the bone at the base of my spine. They have gone so deep and the bones have been so exposed that I have had to be operated on to avoid permanent damage.

You can even get bedsores in the hospital. It made no difference that for three months I was pampered, massaged, and turned over several times a day in the intensive care unit—sores broke out after a fortnight in emergency life support. It took nine months in Kerpape to heal that first attack.

*

THE HOURS, the nights, the months I spent lying on my back, looking up at the ceiling, brought me a treasure that I—diligent pupil of our celebrity-obsessed culture—had never noticed before: silence.

When there's silence, consciousness takes control. It places what surrounds you in context. The self holds court. At first you're a little afraid. There are no sounds to take you anywhere, no sensations to mark the boundaries of your body. Just a vast desert, barren and inert. You have to make yourself minute to discover elements of life in such desolation. But then, finally, you begin to observe the infinitely small. I would notice a nurse's finger returning to the vertical after giving me a painless injection somewhere in the body I couldn't feel anymore; a drop of water rolling from a cold pad down my temple, darting into my ear, tickling me until sleep canceled it; the pressure of the plaster stuck on my nostril to maintain the curve of the oxygen tube; an eyelid fluttering with exhaustion. A face coming closer: sound but nothing comprehensible, no words. The inside of my eyelids, purple under the neon light. My eyes tilting backward as it grew dark. Then nothing, my brain on standby, until a noise or some pressure on my face tentatively woke me up. In those hours when my eyes were shut, some faint activity would start up inside.

One day, I heard a voice. It wasn't mine, it came from inside me. If anything, it was a woman's voice, maybe Béatrice's. It asked me questions as if it were an autonomous entity and when I didn't respond, it answered them too. I got used to it and started to answer—not that I recognized my own voice either. It felt as if two uninvited chatterboxes were having a conversation in my head. They were perfectly entertaining though. It was me after all. Gradually, I asserted myself. I began to stand in for the more masculine voice. At first we talked about strangely anodyne things.

"Do you remember your train of thought?"

"Yes, yes, I think so."

"So, what are you going to say to Béatrice when she comes?"

"I'm just going to look at her. Give me a break!"

My voice and the internal one argued constantly until I couldn't work out who was who anymore.

I looked at the ceiling for months without getting bored. Staring at its dazzling whiteness, I mourned the loss of my body and I returned to the land of the living. I tamed the voice that could have had me certified as a lunatic (all that we needed was for me to be locked up). I forgot the horrific times spent learning how to breathe without a ventilator, how to live with the bits that were left of me and with those they'd added. Buoyed up by all the activity going on inside me, reassured by Béatrice's love, I recovered.

I scrutinized the few sensations I still felt. I prepared for Béatrice's visits with endless internal powwows. I disappeared when she was with me, memorizing her every look, her every word. Her sense of hope was infectious. With her at my side, all of the pieces of my new reality started to come together.

My belief in the future took shape in silence. The hours passed. All I needed to think about was my physical survival.

It was essential I didn't turn my back on hope. I would feel appalling pain in the parts of my body still capable of sensation, which would leave me gasping for breath, blank-eyed. But the moment it abated, hope would appear. And with it, a sense of rebirth.

Silence.

In that catastrophic time I still dared to believe things could change. The gulf between what I was experiencing and the happiness I anticipated strengthened my sense of hope.

Disability and illness fracture and damage the body, but in confronting you with death, they also release a breath of life in the form of hope, which constantly replenishes itself. When you breathe it correctly, you find your second wind.

Marathon runners know about catching a second wind. It's a kind of state of grace. Your breathing relaxes and becomes deeper, all the pain disappears. I had been struggling to breathe for forty-two years. We all suffocate ourselves by rushing too fast, by wanting to be the best, the first. The people who can breathe best after twenty or thirty miles are the ones who imagine reaching their goal. It may be the great supper of God or finding love again, but visualizing getting there is essential.

No one runs a marathon on their own.

When you can see beyond the screams, the whispered confidences, the sterilized beds waiting for their next occupants, you realize humanity is made up of the shades of the dead and their groans. You find out there has been a before and there will be an after, that the ancients shared our world, that eternity is inhabited by those who have come before us. Hope is the bridge that leads from, as Khalil Gibran says in *The Prophet,* "remembrances, the glimmering arches that span the summits of the mind" to eternity

*

THE TELEPHONE rang. A heavenly voice filled the room. "This is Marie-Hélène Mathieu, director of the OCH," the Christian association for people with disabilities. I was definitely getting closer to Heaven. "I saw you on *La Marche du Siècle,* Jean-Marie Cavada's television talk show. I'd like you to be a speaker in one of the lecture series I'm putting on."

"That's very flattering. . . . But I'm not sure I have a great deal of time free. I am hardly a believer myself. And as far as my thoughts on disabilities are concerned, I'm afraid I am still very wet behind the ears."

How could I refuse though? I didn't want to argue. The talk was in three months and, with any luck, events would come to my rescue.

"I'd like my wife, who has been ill for fifteen years, to do the talk with me. The grace of her faith should balance the two of us out nicely."

"What would you like to call your talk?"

I was worn out, didn't have any points of reference, just a flash of insight.

"The second wind."

"Very well, we'll publicize it as 'The Second Wind of Philippe and Béatrice Pozzo di Borgo.'"

"No, it should be 'The Second Wind of Béatrice and Philippe.'"

She was surprised but I stood by the title. It felt as if she was doing me a real service letting me express this intuition.

Why Béatrice and Philippe? When I was at my weakest, I could see how much Béatrice's illness had helped me adapt to my disability. I might have been very far away from everyone at times, but I never lost heart. It wasn't any feeling of guilt toward a woman who had suffered and fought for fifteen years, or misplaced pride, an urge to compete with her. No, she inspired me with the confidence she found within herself. As long as we still had the energy, our lives were beautiful in themselves, and it would be deplorable not to appreciate it. It was just like the look that welcomed me back when I woke up after a month in a coma. How could I express my idea of a second wind without starting with Béatrice? Gradually, over the past year, the suffering and the true joys of life had seeped into me—the pleasure of talking, of beauty. How many nights had I spent lying next to her, thinking, as if she were my key to the truth?

Béatrice was radiant. I kept her company as best I could.

There was nothing outwardly to suggest she was ill. She was just as beautiful, elegant, smiling, optimistic, and attentive as ever. But she couldn't climb stairs anymore and every three months she had to lie down for what seemed like an eternity. She made sure everything seemed normal. Sometimes, in moments of utter exhaustion, she would despair over the fact that no one thought of her as sick. She resented everyone, although really, she was angry with herself most of all for having such a thirst for life. She would have liked to have been able to give up. I'd offer her my shoulder so she could collapse, let it all out, then she'd set off again.

At the lecture, her calm and her smile expressed her entire philosophy. I looked at that room of five hundred people captivated by her strength. No sniffing or coughing. Undivided attention. Her life was laid out for all to see, consistent from the moment she was born and illuminated by her vision of eternity, however great the sacrifice it might demand. What was there for me to say after a display like that, other than that it was very easy to live with a disability if you had such an amazing source of energy by your side, coursing through your immobile self like an electric current?

Without Béatrice, I wouldn't have made any of this effort. During the year I was hospitalized, I discovered a world that had passed me by, a world I had never examined very closely—that of suffering. I had only known Béa's suffering, and that was in private—it wasn't an ugly social fact. When you've been in intensive care units and heard people screaming, when you've experienced the loneliness of a hospital ward, you see things differently. You go beyond words, beyond silence, and discover your humanity. The body, the subject of so many eulogies before then, gradually fades into insignificance compared to a revitalized spirit, a renewed spirituality. You experience a radical change of heart. And you find other people deep within you, in your inner self, the mystery of who you are.

Béatrice's Cypresses

Béatrice was taken to the hospital for the last time. Like a modern-day Carmelite, they put her in a sort of transparent plastic bubble. To enter, I had to go through a decontamination air lock and be dressed from head to toe in sterile cotton first. She was at the end of a corridor. There were three more doors. A disinfected wheelchair was waiting for me. We couldn't be close for two months; our only sight of each other was blurry and distorted by plastic.

Béatrice contracted generalized septicemia. She couldn't eat or drink, water couldn't even pass her lips. She was reduced to dabbing endlessly at her mouth with cotton pads to wipe away the phlegm that clogged it up. I'd be on the other side of the aseptic curtain, keeping her company through this agonizing time.

She told her father, "I saw Christ, you know, Papa. He said to me, 'Wipe your mouth on my cloak, its cloth will erase all sins.'" She patiently picked up another pad of cotton wool. "I have erased all sins."

Wrap yourself in my cloak of tenderness.

Béatrice's last moments on earth were illuminated by an unwavering sense of hope, genuine anticipation.

Three days before she died, they let her out of her plastic bubble. It was too late. Her eyes were already shut. She could barely see. Our children came, each taking a turn sitting on my knees. They sobbed as I talked to them about her, then they went out in their medical disguises.

"Thy will be done," were her last words. Then she sank down a little farther in her bed.

They gave me permission to take her home. The nurses dressed her in her favorite suit. We laid her on the daybed by the fireplace, where she liked to sit when she was tired. Abdel wept. For three days, she was surrounded by family and friends. Céline, our young au pair with red, tear-stained eyes, kept a table stocked with food, which everyone picked at. My father helped to organize the funeral. He told me, in tears, that she had taught him how to pray. Abdel brought her belongings back from the hospital: there were things she'd written, letters. She had kept a logbook.

Every entry emanated gentleness, her love for those close to her, her trust in God, her faith that she would get better. She stubbornly pledged to stay alive until Robert-Jean, her lovely young boy, reached eighteen. When she felt she was slipping away, this same serenity gave her the strength to forgive me, to find words of guidance for Laetitia and consolation for Robert-Jean.

Then she turned to God.

*

I CHOSE the most beautiful coffin I could find and had a cross put on it. We organized a service at the Protestant church and a mass at Dangu. Our children were wonderful. They read the Prayer of St. Augustine, which she used to recite to them in the evening. They wouldn't notice its pathos or see the tears in her eyes; they would just be lulled by the sweetness of her voice, then I would take them up to bed as they were about to fall asleep.

*

AT THE funeral in Dangu, our friends Nicolas and Sophie sang Béatrice's favorite hymn. I sank down in my chair. Robert-Jean held my hand. He started crying. Laetitia put her arm around his shoulder. Béatrice's coffin was covered with the tenderest pink pansies, sent by a friend. The floor was strewn with thousands of white flowers. "Dry your tears and don't cry if you love me."

Béatrice who art in Heaven . . .

*

WE PASSED by the foot of the hill in Dangu; Béatrice's grave was at the top. I could only get to it with Abdel's help. I always felt I was just under her grave, that I could reach her just by raising my arms.

I found it hard to talk about her in the first year after she'd gone, and since. I didn't talk to her at night—I conducted monologues about her—and she didn't take me in her arms when I couldn't sleep.

I felt her floating just above me. Her paradise must have been very close. She was like smoke from a cigarette; she emerged from me and then vanished almost immediately.

She hadn't spoken to me yet. She was still the way she was in the last days of her life, motionless and silent apart from the raspy breaths that barely lifted her chest.

I choked on the words when I tried to talk about her. No sound came out; all I could feel was a burning sensation behind my eyes.

Maybe she was too sad to talk to me?

Abdel occasionally took me up to the cemetery. He pushed me across the uneven ground. The names were gradually fading from the headstones. A few gleaming slabs of marble lettered in gold indicated the latest arrivals. Béatrice was the first of our clan ever to be buried on the mainland. I wanted to keep her near me until I died. Afterward she would go back to Corsica with me. The chapel was never crowded there, the night was full of animation and noises, the smells of the maquis hung in the air, the view was so incredibly beautiful.

Laetitia organized a family gathering at the Dangu cemetery. Everyone came. The children crouched down around her grave. My niece Valentine, who was ten, was the only one who didn't cry; instead she doggedly went around picking up all the flowerpots that had been knocked over by the wind.

When I went up there, I would settle down in front of her grave and feel her presence all around. I sensed her in the gentle rustle of the cypresses. But she disappeared when I went back down the hill. She didn't follow me into the new apartment.

I heard her laugh only once, when a young woman kissed me. It was how she used to laugh when we were alone together in bed, like a happy little girl. She'd forget her body and escape with me like an indulged child. I'd forgotten that laugh in the unbearable tension of the past months.

She had turned her gaze to Heaven and I had followed her.

She used to pray for hours at a time. I tried to melt into her gaze, reliving those unexpectedly joyful moments. She prayed as if she were liberating herself from her suffering. Her joy became everyone's prayer. She raised me up. He existed since she was with Him.

My own feelings were shadows; all that was left was her pain, which I had made mine, and her absence.

Sometimes I would bury myself in my bed for weeks. I would abandon everyone, until I'd hear Robert-Jean wriggling around near me or become aware of Laetitia trying to get me to drink or sense Abdel waiting, comfortably ensconced in my wheelchair. They brought me back to earth. I was surprised how easily I returned. I'd hear myself laughing. I felt proud of my children. But I wasn't worried about rejoining Béatrice either, it was even a source of relief. There were terrible moments: I wanted to float away but the others held me back.

I do not know which way to go anymore. Perhaps with time, with my children, with their children, with a woman . . . Perhaps this rocking chair will come to a standstill after all.

*

BÉA HAD gone. Laetitia and Robert-Jean were still here. The four of us had been happy together.

When the pain was at its most acute, I thought all my defenses would give way, that my head would explode: my eyes had already rolled upward, my body was arched back, I hadn't spoken for ages. In an act of desperation, I would cut myself off from everything. I would disappear into my unconscious with just one obsession: to hold on once again for our beloved children.

I felt alone in my bed for the first time the day Béatrice's mother told me that there was nothing left to be done, whatever the doctors said. There was nothing left. Nothing of Béatrice's wonderful presence except a constant ache in the back of my throat. Nothing of the man of action who had been broken by losing her, rather than by his disability. All that remained was worrying about the children. I stayed in bed. The house went to hell. Céline, the au pair, didn't give a damn anymore. Nor did I. There were only a few people who still came to see the three of us. My parents-in-law, of course; my sister-in-law Anne-Marie; a few old girlfriends who ran out of steam when confronted with my depression.

The rest of the family was very circumspect, anesthetized by our silence and by their shame. The only sounds during the day were the children moving about; Aunt Éliane's witty and compassionate phone call at ten past nine; Abdel's mayhem; the nurses in the morning (and with some of them, I didn't even open my eyes); and Sabrya, the nurse who'd become a friend.

I loved Béatrice. As the days went by, I found things she had written. Apart from a few drafts of letters to me when I was on long trips abroad, all I found were accounts of her suffering. Almost twenty-five years of incredible, defiant happiness together, so many things in which we innocently, magnificently took delight—and now all that was left were catastrophic pages of loneliness and doubt.

When her mother died, Laetitia read what she'd written and was devastated. I found snatches of horror scrawled on loose sheets of paper and in two small notebooks, one green and one red. If only I had never seen them. They were like a black border around every moment of happiness in our lives.

*

AFTER I'D read one of her laments, I stayed in bed for days. I had been blinded by pride. I never knew. They became virtually all I thought about. During the day I had them taped to the board above my bed; at night, I couldn't bear them being on my bedside table. I wanted to turn away from them, to Béatrice's side of the bed, but I could only lean my head and let the tears flow.

They were never dated precisely. All told, they barely filled twenty pages. Every word was a cry of despair. Some passages reminded me of moments I had forgotten about. They revealed the heartbreak of a great beauty who could only have miscarriages and stillbirths; the anxiety of a woman consumed by an invisible cancer, a woman who was so beautiful in everyone else's eyes and yet aware that she was rotting inside; the exhaustion of a human being who longed so much for what she couldn't have. And then, her energy spent, she had to suffer the ultimate insult when the man she still loved broke his neck on the hard ground, the same ground she wished would lay gently on her when her time came.

She was transformed from a sorrowful, loving soul into a pietà, burdened by the weight of a shattered body. She, the crucified woman, resurrected me. The irony. She was buried under her smile. Meanwhile I raced off in every direction to escape her bleeding legs, her putrid blood, her struggle to survive. But I'd always come back to take her in my arms again on her huge bed, wouldn't I, smiling bitterly at a grace that hid so many tears, at the woman who had deserved compassion for so many years.

*

I DECIDED to return to Crest-Voland, find the place where I crashed, and, in some way, try to exorcise the accident by flying from there again in my wheelchair. Childish, I know. But my real friends were those crazy, magnificent flying men Béa never really liked. They were overwhelmed by feelings of guilt and I wanted to relieve them. I longed to catch a thermal that would take me fifteen or twenty thousand feet. I'd talk to my wife out loud up there, as I sometimes did at night. In the splendor of the mountain, I'd feel closer to her. I sometimes had an obscure feeling of wanting to join her, just as I'd been tempted to leave her after the accident. It was irrational and childish.

I also liked the thought of Abdel on a two-man flight, screaming at whoever would listen that it wasn't his idea.

*

MY FRIENDS fitted a special seat that inflated when the wing picked up speed and should cushion my landing. Yves, hanging behind my harness, had the controls. We had decided that I would give him instructions by moving my head. Head left: turn at the indicated angle; head down: brake; head up: release the brakes. We flew three times. The whole team carried us and gave us speed for takeoff. Tilting my head down slightly, I signaled to Yves that a bit of brake was needed, then we were airborne.

I rediscovered the sensation of flight, or at least my head did—I couldn't feel anything with the rest of my body. We flew our usual route. At one point, Yves yelled at me that I was taking too much of a risk: we were too close to the forest. But I knew that, by skimming the treetops, we would have enough small parcels of hot air to keep us aloft and could pick up the ridge a few hundred yards away, see the whole Albertville valley, dive in, and then bounce off the summit. Yves hesitated, but I indicated that he had to follow me. Suddenly, we'd caught a fantastic thermal. We were in the elevator! In a few seconds we had gone up hundreds of feet. We were above the peak, wheeling in great circles. What an amazing sight! We tried to regain altitude, but the conditions wouldn't allow it, so we dived back down to the forest. We followed birds, chased other wings. We could have stayed up there forever, but Yves gestured that we had to go back. We'd been flying for more than an hour and a half. I didn't feel any tiredness. It felt like a resurrection. We passed the last rocky outcrop and raced toward the chalet. To maintain the spirit of mature, good sense in which the enterprise had been conducted thus far, I steered Yves toward the hill above the chalet and asked him to do some hedge-hopping. We came zigzagging down the hillside, less than nine feet off the ground. What a feeling! Yves lined us up to land against a nice headwind. Suddenly, just as we were about to touch down, the wind changed direction. We were sent hurtling at over twenty-five miles an hour. I didn't have any legs to help him; we wiped out. My face acted as a brake. After plowing up the ground for thirty yards or so, we came to a standstill and burst out laughing, which made all our friends who'd come to watch start laughing too. My face was covered in blood. I bore the marks of that landing for several weeks, but I can't describe how relieved I felt.

When I got back to Paris, I said something about a wheelchair accident. Apart from Laetitia, no one suspected my irresponsibility.

Corsican Soul

IT WAS ONLY a few months after Béatrice's death, and I was in Corsica, in the tower framed by the mountains, a place she loved intensely. The shutters in my bedroom had been pulled. I could feel the shadows lengthening in my mind. I had started trying to do some dictation the day before, but the tape deck hadn't recorded anything. Tears of tiredness, sadness, and resignation had welled up behind my sunglasses.

My cousin Nouns had come. He had tried to make me laugh and talk about flying in my wheelchair, last month's recidivism, but I clung to my sadness, my eyes burning. I drowsed until a cold breeze coming down off the mountain woke me. The tinkling of a bell: a neighbor's cow. I called out. Françoise, the housekeeper, came in, shouting. I didn't have the strength to talk to her about Béatrice, even though she had independently organized a mass in her memory in nearby Alata while we were burying her on the mainland. I'd said we'd look at the photos together another time. She listed the people who'd expressed their affection for Beatrice, then told me how, when she had moved here twenty years ago after the death of her only daughter, the remoteness of these Corsican mountains had been a lifeline to her. I knew that was true but I found it painful. She brought me a bottle of her homemade peach liqueur, which Beatrice and I used to love drinking with her so much, but I could only taste the bitterness of the peach stones. We looked at the valley together. Two buzzards wheeled on the horizon, they must have found a thermal. It was such a still evening, gradually even the cow stopped chewing. Water splashed in the fountain. The light blurred. A few hundred feet below lay the family's funerary chapel, which had always been such a source of great pride to me. I used to say it was good to know where we'd be spending eternity. One of those things it's easy to say.

The sound of my heart pounding in my brain became steadily louder until it was unbearable. My blood pressure was over twenty, I was drenched in sweat, I didn't know what was wrong with me anymore. Why wouldn't the pain stop? Why couldn't I just talk about Béatrice and fall asleep in peace up here in the mountains? One fit of convulsions followed the next. Céline sat at the foot of my wheelchair as I writhed around. She offered to read me the novel I'd been meaning to start. Despite the seizures, I still caught a few passages about Rimbaud, Verlaine, Longfellow. So much of what happens to us is blind chance.

I shut my eyes. Céline stayed with me. She picked up her

airport novel. I felt calmer—the presence of a young woman, however unlike Béatrice, had its effect on me. She could have taken my hand, I wouldn't have held it against her. Abdel had given me a pill to help me sleep. I felt myself slipping away, sinking through waves of darkness.

The rattle in my lungs woke me up. Slowly I made out the sounds in the house, the children bustling about. I had forgotten about them. The world came back to me in an instant—in the hoarse crackle of fluid in my chest. I didn't dare call out in case I sounded a discordant note in that cheerful hive of activity. Gradually I remembered the scenes before I'd fallen asleep. Abdel had made a hash of things lifting me onto the bed, and I had felt myself going over backward in my wheelchair. I had been terrified this would be my last fall. All I had was my head; I hadn't had anything to protect it. Abdel had braced himself to cushion the blow. I had heard my head hit the floor. From the sound of the impact, I had known this wasn't the last time. My cousin Nouns had come in to give a hand in his usual good-humored way. He had seen me lying on my back, my legs still entangled in my wheelchair, and had commented, "Not really the time for a knee trembler, is it?" I was so far gone that I hadn't even known what that had meant. I had laughed and cried at the same time. He had sat me up, then lifted me onto the bed; I had flopped over on the pressure sore mattress. I would have happily drowned in it.

When he realized that I was awake, Abdel tried a new technique to sit me upright. A misguided effort. As he picked me up under my shoulders, my arms went flying and smashed into the roughly plastered walls. Two of my fingers burst like ripe fruit, blood spurting everywhere. I started crying. I couldn't feel anything, it didn't hurt, I was just crying. I didn't belong to myself anymore, my body was falling to pieces. I couldn't cope.

I wanted to start talking to Béatrice, but I was overwhelmed with anxiety. I felt I wasn't wanted down here on earth, that I should make myself scarce. I was going to die alone in that bed. The pressure built up in my head again. I didn't want to leave right away. I focused on my halting breathing and tried as hard as I could to exhale the air backed up in my lungs. The spasms were coming constantly, I was all stiff and cold, as if I'd already kicked the bucket.

Abdel got me dressed. I asked him to put me under the lime tree by the fountain. Two acacias framing the landscape had bloomed again after a fire three years before. Occasionally, there was the pounding of a hammer: workmen were restoring the château.

The sea air had been eating away at the crumbling château for a century and flames had played around it several times, but in 1978 its roof caught fire. Water planes were mobilized, but they couldn't do anything. Hundreds of firemen fought to save this historic building. Three found themselves surrounded by flames. The youngest tried to run for it, unlike his more experienced colleagues. He was soon caught. He died a few hundred yards from where I was sitting. I could see the plaque laid in his memory on the roadside below. There was a ceremony every August 7 with Alata village's brass band, the municipal fire brigade, the mayor, some other officials, and our family. Oh, that poor firefighter lying sadly by the Duke of Pozzo di Borgo's road. He didn't care if one of the Pozzos was remembering him. He would rather have lived. He was stuck between the surviving Pozzos in the tower and the dead ones in the chapel.

The bell rang in my ears again. I didn't know what the tape deck was going to record out of all this noise and my delusions. I sensed the cow right behind me, but couldn't turn around. I thought it was amused by the sight of this invalid talking to himself. Don't worry, old thing, it will be your turn soon. Our mountain was covered with the dead.

An army helicopter passed in the distance, like the one that had come looking for me on a paragliding expedition some years before. The family was having a picnic on the beach, so I had decided to paraglide down from Punta, just above the château, and join them. I hadn't worked out a route. I just saw a point and thought I could fly over it and then down to the beach. I set off at six in the evening in a pair of shorts, a vest, and running shoes. I came down past the point in nine-foot tall scrub, and, folding up my wing, crawled along what looked like a boar's tracks. I thought I'd be able to set off from the next peak, but after an hour's painful progress, I found myself on a point that clearly did not overlook the beach I was looking for.

It was too late to turn around. The only thing I could do was to spend the night out in the open, wrapped up in my wing on a rock.

I found out later that Béatrice had called the police.

"So, how old is your son?"

"It's my husband!"

"Ah, madam . . . Are you telling me your husband's never come home in the early hours of the morning?"

Her insisting was of no use, they still told her to call back at six in the morning. Then they sent a helicopter to rescue me. I was taken to the hospital—where they checked to see that I had no broken bones, just a few superficial cuts—and then they were kind enough to take me home. I had a quick shower and put on a suit and tie to go to a meeting with the company president in Paris. I barely had time to see Béatrice, exhausted from her all-night vigil. She couldn't breathe for a moment when I kissed her and said, "See you tomorrow, darling."

*

I RETREATED into myself that evening. I tried to use my body's pain to gauge its boundaries. My head was relatively pain-free, although it felt slightly constricted—allergies were making my face and neck itch and my shoulders were spasming constantly. The right shoulder had become decalcified because of the impact of the crash. They'd tried calcium injections for six months, which made me feverish and nauseous at night and left me punch-drunk. "You must have had a bad fall," the doctor said. Was that a joke or the detachment of the specialist who didn't see beyond his X-rays? The right shoulder sometimes hurt very badly. No one could touch me. I'd hold my breath and close my eyes, knowing it would pass, that I'd just have to wait a minute or two. "No big deal, I've known worse. Yes, yes, it'll go, I promise. No, no, don't touch me. Don't touch my shoulder!" My shoulders would make all my nerves go haywire. Sometimes the burning feeling was so terrible I would ask to lie in a darkened room. I would think of Rimbaud's foolish virgin in *A Season in Hell*: "I really am suffering . . . a little cool air, Lord, please."

In Marcus Aurelius, I read: "God grant me the serenity to accept the things I cannot change. Courage to change the things that I can. And wisdom to know the difference."

*

LYING IN the dark of my room, I caught a stomach-churning whiff of preparations in the kitchen. We were entertaining forty Corsicans from the mountains the following day. It had been a long time since the Pozzos had entertained in style. Abdel was in charge of operations and had planned a barbecue. He had gone down to choose a sheep from a neighboring shepherd that afternoon. He had been surprised by the scrawny aspect of the flock, but in the end had made do with a seventy-pound ewe. I was downstairs when he came back and unloaded the animal. Three of its legs were tied together, the fourth free. He went off to get some knives. I wasn't sure I wanted to be there. I thought about Béatrice. The sheep reminded me of her—sentenced to death—and of me too, with my paralysis. The animal tried to drag itself along on its fourth leg but only succeeded in turning in a circle. How often had I dreamed of escaping from my paralysis? How often had I dreamed of being able to pick Béatrice up from one of her hospital beds so she could be close to me, in our bed, so she could pass away in my arms? The medical butchers kept her to the end. They finished her off. How could she have endured so much torment without ever complaining? She fought against the doctors and their power all her life.

Abdel felt for the carotid vein, then slit the ewe's throat in one sharp movement. Bright red blood spurted out, the color of strawberry juice. Suddenly I remembered Béatrice's breathing at the end of life, and realized they'd killed her long before I'd guessed. The ewe had started doing that same jerky breathing—eyes closed, limbs not moving, only its crushed chest heaving up and down in short, brutal shudders. Then it lay completely still for a long while, until Abdel announced it would enter its death throes in one minute. Its free leg started shaking all over the place—spasming, we both realized—just like my shuddering, uncontrolled limbs. It convulsed in one violent, final movement, and then Abdel confidently untied the other three legs. Using a rope, he hung the animal over a tarp, then went to get Françoise to take some family photos. We arranged ourselves under the lime tree near the fountain. Françoise took a picture of us: Abdel, the ewe, and me.

He slid a rod into one of its legs, between the skin and the flesh, then blew into it as if it were a bagpipe. The animal inflated like a balloon, tripling in size. Once this was done, he asked Françoise to pass him a piece of string to tie up the leg, then began hitting the animal. The thuds resonated around the tower. He was relentless, like a metronome. After tenderizing the meat, Abdel took his knife and began to cut the animal up. In less than ten minutes, it was stripped down to the bone. Then all that was left was to gut it and collect the offal to cook the vegetables, hence the acrid smell filling my room that evening.

The Sanguinaires Islands

LYING ON MY back in the position I'd been in for three days, my eyes closed, something seemed different. I wasn't suffering anymore. I hardly dared believe it: I didn't feel any pain.

At seven in the morning, I called to Abdel. He sprang up like a robot; he hadn't slept for three days either. "Abdel, put on some Schubert, please." I was finding it hard to breathe but that didn't matter. I wasn't in pain anymore. Abdel brought me breakfast.

"Abdel, will you read me a psalm, please?"

The gist was familiar: God is kind. There is a way to salvation for all those who suffer. But I didn't understand, I was exhausted. I found it hard to fathom those words, which seemed so certain of their meaning.

The party began on Thursday night. We had dinner and then went through to the great guardroom to listen to the singers from Alata. There was so much grief in their songs: the Arabic tones, the high-pitched keening, and the deep bass voices echoing the vibrations of the mountain and the cries of the buzzards circling and wheeling overhead. I was tired, but I couldn't bring myself to leave the room. They were singing for me, for Béatrice. I had requested "Salve Regina." The voices swelled. I withdrew into myself. Béatrice loved that hymn. They looked at me as they sang, their left hands cupping their ears, their voices echoing around. The emotion exhausted me. When they left, I hadn't really eaten, I hadn't spoken, all I'd heard was that Corsican polyphony. A shepherd bowed and kissed my hand. Abdel didn't take me to bed until late. I was shivering with fever and didn't sleep much.

FOR THE first time since arriving in Corsica ten days earlier, I decided to tag along with the children when they went to the beach. My cousin Barbara; her husband, Philip; and their six children were at the Pozzos' usual place, a cove the family had been camping alongside for thirty years. Just like Granny twenty years before her, Barbara was doing a tapestry in the shade of an awning while keeping an eye on the troops. I settled in next to her for the afternoon, and found myself remembering the beaches of my childhood.

My friend François had been left paralyzed by a little wave not unlike the ones that afternoon. He had been swimming with his wife and family, his children merrily splashing each other, when a slightly bigger wave had knocked them over. They all got up—roaring with laughter—except François, who stayed facedown in the water. They thought he was pretending. When they realized he wasn't breathing, they carried him up onto the beach. He had fractured his first and second cervical vertebrae. Thanks to his faith and his family's love, he held on for seven years without leaving his bed. The doctors couldn't believe it. Then he died.

I raised my eyes to the horizon. The Sanguinaires islands were silhouetted against the sky. Legend had it that they were named after the plague victims, with their "black blood," who were shipped there during the four centuries of Genoese rule, from the fifteenth to the eighteenth century. Another tradition said it was because the setting sun dyed them blood red. I thought of you, Béatrice. Death carried off those plague sufferers too. They were burnt at the stake, then their ashes were scattered on those parched, sterile islands.

Barbara looked up from what she was working on to check on the next generation. All was well. "Don't worry, little cousin, you and Béatrice will be together again." I looked at Abdel playing with the children down on the beach. Laetitia was reveling in the hot sun. Her hair was gleaming black, her skin white. She was a woman now. Barbara's brood gamboled and frolicked. We were all going to meet up later on the huge beach at Capo di Feno.

Abdel moved me to the small car. Robert-Jean squeezed in the back to hold me steady on corners. We reached the restaurant, Chez Pierretou, a shack on the vast, beautiful, dangerous stretch of beach. My crack team carried me across the sand and set me down at the head of the table. The children, who had the sea to themselves, swam naked. I let myself sink into a state of torpor, lulled by the surf. It grew dark, and I shrank down in my wheelchair. A few young women smiled and said hello to me. I dozed until the children came and sat around the long table under the palm trees. Cousin Philip took charge. Spaghetti with octopus—the octopus had been caught off the beach that afternoon—and a table wine from the interior of the island in unlabeled bottles. The children chattered away, stuffing themselves, except for young François, who was sulking at being banished to the end of the table. I told him to come and sit between his father and me, which he did, lisping through a big smile. He was the most sensitive of Barbara's children. The others were Marie, with the raunchy language of a sixteen-year-old; Titou, the youngest, with his big, googly eyes; and Josephine, with whom Robert-Jean was in love, just as the rest of us were with her mother. The children got up to get ice creams and disappeared into the night. How many times had we come here with Béatrice? She and I spent the night here once on our own. She was happy. We were warm, waking up every now and then to the roar of the surf.

Around midnight, I started shaking violently. I told Abdel it was time to pick up sticks, then withdrew into myself. The pain took hold. I had experienced something like it the year before when Béatrice was still alive, but now I was alone. It was just a stupid, mechanical pain, a bladder outlet obstruction. The catheter was blocked and the urine had been forced back through the kidneys and into the blood. It went up to the brain, and then you exploded. It was idiotic. That was how Béatrice had gone in three days. I held out for five minutes, then gave in and howled like an animal.

It felt like all the blood vessels in my brain had burst. I couldn't see anything and I couldn't breathe. Abdel struggled with the piping for three hours. Now and then the catheter would clear, my blood pressure would go down from thirty to twelve, my brain could breathe again. I'd start to think it was all over, then another tremor would wipe me out.

Abdel spent the night draining crap out of my bladder with syringes. In the morning, I was covered in sweat, the bed was soaked, and the pain flared up again. I wanted to be with Béatrice, I stopped responding to anything. Abdel called an ambulance. There was no solution. I just had to wait, endure, not rebel, brace myself when there was a moment's respite, and give in when it started again.

There was only one doctor on weekend duty at the hospital. It was mayhem. The nurses were happy to have a Pozzo though. They told me about the old days, events they'd attended at the château. The doctor raised the possibility of an operation, but Abdel countered with a campaign of passive resistance. They decided to put me under observation. Sweat poured off me continually. There was another scare at eight o'clock. Then the doctor sent me back up the mountain by ambulance. Abdel put me to bed. I had a terrible night. The next morning we kept changing our minds about whether to go back. Finally Abdel rang and asked them to send a larger diameter catheter. I was still sweating, but I could stand it for a good half a day.

In the midst of all this, my sister Alexandra had arrived with her son. I stayed in bed, unable even to say hello to them. At two o'clock in the morning, I had another violent attack. I couldn't remember ever having experienced such futile agony, like a woman giving birth to a stillborn child. Béatrice had gritted her teeth in pain and fury with our first child. I screamed my head off. Alexandra moved up to a room at the top of the tower. Laetitia joined her, sobbing. Abdel wouldn't let anyone into my room as he desperately tried to get things moving. An hour later, it had passed, but I was shaking all over, and I couldn't shut my mouth. To Abdel's consternation, I also couldn't speak, as I was too busy concentrating on not biting my tongue. I breathed in short, shallow bursts. It took several hours for my body to calm down. Abdel let me sleep in the next morning. At one o'clock, our Bastia cousins arrived on cue. I asked Abdel to put me in my chair.

"Corsica's going to the dogs," Antoine declared mournfully. I followed the conversation from afar. Alexandra was listening, so I could rest in my damn wheelchair in my hat and sunglasses, swathed in a djellaba. I felt dizzy, big drops of sweat rolled out from under the hat. Hélène, Antoine's wife, noticed. I was determined to stay to the end as a mark of respect for my friends from the North. Hélène—a delicate

woman with a pretty face resting on a thin, elongated neck—
had had a bone marrow transplant a few years before, which
had cured her cancer. She had been a brave, compassionate
friend to Béatrice at the end of her life. Beautiful and quiet,
she observed the world through her deep-set eyes. Meanwhile,
her husband analyzed the political situation and enjoyed the
local wild boar that Françoise had prepared.

I SENT for the stonemason because I wanted to replace the
temporary slab on Béatrice's grave with one made from pink
Corsican marble. He was a striking figure, with a small head,
gaunt face, bushy red beard, and a sparkling wit. He had been
working on gravestones for twenty-eight years. I found his serenity and sense of humor refreshing. I told him about my
childhood memories of his fellow stonecutters at the exit of
Ajaccio's marine cemetery. Back then, there were about fifty
masons competing with one another. Now he was the last one
in Corsica. He was proud of it, but he wasn't going to pass on
his expertise to his son: "There's no future in stonecutting."

*

IN THE end, the temporary slab was replaced with a mosaic
I commissioned from Alexandra. It had a pattern of yellow
chrysanthemums and purple irises, Béatrice's favorite combi-
nation.

Sabrya

ONE MOMENT BÉATRICE had been lying on the daybed and the body snatchers had been coming to take her away. . . . Then months had passed, depression had set in, and I had surrendered.

When Béatrice danced she made my head spin. Later I kept her on her feet even though her legs were covered in wounds. Were our rhythms ever really in sync?

In that frantic race, I was never really in tune with her faltering energy.

*

THAT MORNING, just like every morning in Paris, a young nurse came to take care of me for a couple of hours. It was a stranger today, though. She said her name was Sabrya. It meant "patience" in Arabic.

She was the same age as Béatrice had been when I met her. I confused the two of them, even though Sabrya had brown hair; velvety, dark, almond-shaped eyes; and smooth skin the color of apricots.

From then on I'd wait for her every morning. When I heard her arrive, I'd shut my eyes, red from grief and insomnia, and let her open them. She did this for several months. Then she'd shave me, moving her face close to mine, and I'd close my eyes again and focus on her delicate hands as they released the tensions of the night. Her scent intoxicated me. I'd want her to stay with me until I fell asleep.

"YOU MUST tell me you admire me a little one day. Come closer, I want to say something to you."

"No, I know what you are going to say."

"Please, Sabrya. Come here, Sabrya. Tell me one day that you love me a bit, with one of your little smiles. Are you going? No, Sabrya, give me another cigarette, stay for another three minutes. Please, Sabrya."

"No, I'm going, I have other patients."

"Sabrya, one more kiss please. I want to give you another one behind your ear."

"No, not behind the ear, it tickles too much—just on the cheek."

She bent down to me. Sensuous, fragrant bliss.

She told me she had twenty different perfumes. I never noticed, it was always the same scent.

"You'll tell me if you love me a little."

"I'll let you know, I promise."

She left with a big smile on her face, saying, "I'll call you."

"Oh! Sabrya, turn out the lights, please."

In time, though, I won her around. She'd keep me company when she wasn't working, sitting cross-legged on my bed—a tiny, delicate soul—while I talked to her about Béatrice or the life she had in front of her. I hid the feelings of excitement she stirred in me. When she talked, all I could see were her full, well-defined lips, her dazzling teeth, her mischievous tongue. I imagined her kissing me. I daydreamed.

One night I invited her to dinner at a fashionable restaurant in Paris. Her mother escorted her. Both were exquisitely dressed. Sabrya wore a yellow suit, her shiny black hair pulled back. I saw the curve of her knees for the first time. Saadia, her mother, was swathed in rich, gold-sequined fabrics, predominantly red and orange. They studied the alien, glitzy world of the restaurant with curiosity.

Saadia was silent; Sabrya and I said our usual playful, tender things. She was raising her glass of Coca-Cola to her lips when, without changing tone, I asked, "Sabrya, will you marry me?" She looked down at her plate, her cheeks flushed. I saw tears. Saadia questioned her. No answer. I would never get an answer.

Saadia invited me to dinner in their small flat in a high-rise in the fifteenth arrondissement. Abdel got all the teenagers hanging around in the yard to help carry me to the cramped lift, folded up my wheelchair, then held me up bodily. We still had another half-landing to climb when we got out of the lift, with me flopped over him like a disjointed puppet. He hauled me up to the top floor, then left me in a tiny living room crowded with pouffes and a television that was on constantly. Sabrya made the tagine while Saadia came and sat next to me. She said a great deal that went over my head until, as I tried to sit up, she stopped me and said, "You know, Mr. Pozzo, I saw her come home a few months ago and she was very happy. She told me she was in love."

I didn't say anything. She'd told her mother one day that she was in a good mood, that she was surprised someone could love her. Maybe there was still some truth in that fleeting confession? Saadia began telling me that it was traditional in her country for the mother to go with the daughter to her new home. Sabrya interrupted her with her usual mischievous smile: "Mom, that's enough!" Her golden neck bent down close to me. We had a very jolly evening—all three of us— and then after dinner, I suggested to Sabrya that we go for a walk. In the anonymous Parisian night, I took her through the virtually deserted streets in my electric wheelchair. She rode sidesaddle, sitting on my knees. I could feel the softness of her left arm round my neck, the caress of her hair on my face. With my chin, I rode my steed at top speed down the middle of the road, all lights blazing. She laughed and sang to me, but didn't mention my dreams about us being together. I whispered sweet things to her, "I love your curls after you've gone swimming, the way your hair is naturally. I know you hate it because you think it looks ethnic. You realize you spend an hour a day pulling your hair back? It shows your face more, of course, but you should still let your curls down. Yes, I know you have ridiculously tiny breasts, and saddlebags—they suit you, your jeans hug every inch. I can see your rounded knees. I feel how soft your arm is round my neck. . . ." She interrupted me with a peal of laughter as a car overtook us.

Board Meeting

THE SUMMER HEAT wave had hit Paris. The burning sensation in my body was becoming unbearable. I had a temperature of a hundred and four degrees. Even my face, which had been spared until then, was on fire. I had blisters everywhere and my scalp was one big scab. Only my ankles, by some trick of my damaged spine, seemed to have any lightness. I felt completely out of my depth. When Laetitia came to sit on my bed to tell me her holiday plans, I broke down and asked her to look after her younger brother. I had to go to the hospital; I couldn't cope anymore.

She reacted exactly as Béatrice would have. She told my friends, and they took me to the Saint-Jean-de-Malte Center, a brand new center for the severely disabled in the middle of Paris. I had followed its construction from start to finish. I was Mr. Disabled—the person to consult—as far as the city bigwigs, the regional council, and the center's donors were concerned. Three months earlier—after the director had put the finishing touches to the project—I had gone there to show Sabrya around. We had been given lunch in the cafeteria, surrounded by people with disabilities of every sort. Sabrya hadn't said a word, terrified by such a weight of misery.

I was put in a studio apartment with a kitchenette, living room, and bathroom. It was on the ground floor, and opened onto a tree-lined patio. All the residents had their own apartments, and they could even live there with their families if they so chose. It took me three days to realize where I was.

My caregivers, Fabienne and Emmanuella, pampered me unstintingly. I appreciated their sweetness. Fabienne was a green-eyed West Indian beauty. Her grandfather was from Brittany, so I called her "the Breton." She lived alone with her six-year-old daughter. Emmanuella was young and pretty, from Guadeloupe. Her scarlet lipstick got me going again. Then there was Brigitte. Residents were divided into two camps: those who thought Brigitte was the most beautiful member of staff, and those who plumped for Foule, a wonderful Senegalese woman. I favored Foule, although everyone who worked there was incredibly sweet, even little Nicole. She could be grumpy, but she always smiled at me, always had something comforting to say.

Although the pain didn't relent, the girls got me sitting up and I had meals on the ward. I didn't eat anything, but I was with the other residents, which was the main thing.

Their number included John Paul, a quadriplegic my

age, whose face was swollen like mine because of allergic re-
actions. Armand, though I didn't know what he was doing
there. He could walk and I saw him swimming like an
Olympic champion in the pool one day. But he definitely had
a problem: he would eat up to five hunks of meat every meal,
his hands trembling. Jean-Marc, a twenty-eight-year-old
from Martinique, who was married with two children. We
became friends. He had just had an accident, but the look
in his eyes radiated optimism. He made us laugh, cheered us
up. He was the only person who had his wife and children
stay in his apartment.

There was a little woman who walked with a stick. I
couldn't tell how old she was, but I got the impression she
wasn't going to leave the establishment again if she could help
it. Corinne, a forty-year-old redhead whose face was entirely
expressionless—apart from a flicker of something in her
eyes—was an alcoholic. Eva from Poland, who kept her head
bowed the whole time, suffered from pain like mine. She had
stopped believing anything could change.

Eric, who was just a boy, was busy writing a life plan for
the director. He wanted to go around to schools giving presen-
tations. With the laborious delivery of cerebral palsy sufferers,
he talked to me at length about the despair he felt. He often
wanted to kill himself, but didn't dare because his father and
three brothers said he didn't have the right.

Michel, a sagging giant, had a weeping right eye, which
drooped in one direction or another, and his body with it. He

spoke in a slow whisper. The caregivers were tough on him because he could have managed by himself but lacked the willpower. He and Eric hated each other. I think they were in love with the same woman. Eric would threaten to sock him, despite the fact that his hands curled inward at the wrists, whereupon Michel —silently and infinitely slowly—would extend one of his huge arms to its full length.

M. Baillet was obsessed about the backboard fitted to his electric wheelchair. He would adjust its angle every minute with the index finger on his right hand. He spent the whole day oscillating between the horizontal and the vertical positions. He used to joke that his calcium levels were going up so fast that he was being turned into a fossil as we spoke. His only means of escape, he would say, was to keep shaking himself up like a bottle of Orangina. He never complained. The nurses told me he was in horrendous pain.

Another resident, a great lug weighing more than three hundred and twenty pounds, was incredibly violent. He'd hold both his arms out stiffly in front of himself and then start banging the table with them, and throwing his body backward and forward. The girls were afraid of him. He never said a word, but his huge red face and bulging eyes were constantly demanding more food. He was flanked by "the brothers," as I called them: two terminal patients whose heads were supported by plastic collars. They had almost no body, just atrophied bones. Their necks were no thicker than a finger, and each had a trach that looked like a grotesque bow tie.

They always had a gentle expression in their eyes. The week before, there had been three of them.

M. Carron, a quadriplegic like me, complained that he was in pain. It frightened him and he asked to be moved to the hospital in Garches. He went, came back, and died early the next morning. We saw him go past on a stretcher, a blanket pulled over his face. The meat eater said he must be dead, otherwise they wouldn't have done that with the blanket. Someone else said it was better that way because he wasn't in pain anymore.

And that is only a few of my brothers and sisters: there were so many others that I haven't mentioned. I felt better when I was with them.

They had settled in for the long haul. They were surprised to see me just passing through, like a tourist, ready to leave at any moment. I promised I'd be back.

*

I WENT to wait for Sabrya in the foyer, after spending all morning resting. The receptionist, a blond Portuguese woman, already had an honor guard of three other wheelchairs. Sabrya arrived wearing a pastel floral dress, transparent to just above her round knees, and beige shoes with a slight heel. A white bra strap hugged one of her tanned shoulders. Her hair was pulled back. She noticed me immediately, but only smiled at the others, saying hello to everyone in her childlike, playful voice. We set off toward the Parc des Buttes-Chaumont. I steered my electric wheelchair with a tennis ball contraption under my chin, which was connected directly to the motor and back wheels. Sabrya walked on my right. I took care to adjust the angle of the ball so she stayed level with me. Her hair gleaming in the sunshine, she laughed at all my sallies with infectious cheerfulness. When I went too far, she would give me a little wink, as if she were giving my hands a friendly pat. We went in by the gates at the bottom of the hill. I threw back my head, looked into her eyes, and told her another stupid, romantic thing. Every now and then she'd stamp her foot and, laughing, say "Stop, stop," or "Philippe, that is enough!"

When we paused halfway up the hill, I wasn't in pain anymore. I claimed my kisses from the previous days. She planted them stingily on the corner of my eyes. We finally got to the top of the park, and sat on the terrace of the restaurant there. She moved her chair alongside mine and looked into my eyes. Our faces were close. We didn't lift our heads.

A curly-haired child came our way without looking at us.

"Sabrya, I have got some things to tell you. We'll go and sit by ourselves under a tree in a moment, and you'll help me."

Her eyes darkened.

"Tell me, Philippe."

"No, in a moment, I'm too nervous."

A waiter took our order. He put the food on the table behind us; we didn't touch it. We carried on batting affectionate remarks back and forth, making each other laugh. Then Sabrya laid her arm on mine. She wanted to know.

We went over to a tree that stood off to one side by itself. Children were playing on the lawn below; swans lazed on the pond beyond a flower bed. I moved the ball away from my chin. Sabrya sat on my lap, her arm around my neck. With great tact, she said she wanted to tell me about herself.

She had guessed what was troubling me.

She told me about her childhood in a village in the middle of nowhere, about the father she hated for his cruelty and the brutal way he treated her mother. She often ran away with her little brother to protect him, knowing that when she returned she would find her mother in tears, covered with bruises.

When she was five years old, her mother was seven months pregnant; she was expecting twins. One evening, her father threw an even more violent fit than usual. Saadia was frightened for her children's sake and set off with them and a suitcase into the night. She wanted to escape, to join her sister in France. At dawn, they were waiting for the Casablanca train on the station platform. Her father found them in the dull light, rushed at his wife, knocked her to the ground, and started pummeling her. Sabrya dragged her screaming brother away. Saadia was yelling at people to save her babies. She lost them both.

Even now, talking about it made Sabrya cry. She was never going to see her father again; she was afraid of men.

She said that I was the first man to talk to her kindly, with respect; that she didn't want to hurt my feelings; and that, most of all, she didn't want to lose me. The more she talked, the less I dared address the issue I had raised that evening at the restaurant. She was looking for a father, and I was dreaming of a girlfriend.

I tried a shy, "Sabrya, I wish we could be together."

She took her arm off my neck, leaned forward slightly, and stared, her hands resting on her knees. When I was with her, when my heart was racing, I forgot that I was twice her age and that she had never thought of me as a lover.

I thought of my death. "I'll live until I'm seventy-five years old, which is not very much in our family of nonagenarians. You'll see our grandchildren born in my lifetime." I told her sadly that if it only depended on my heart, I would wait for her. But I couldn't guarantee my body. Then the pain enveloped me like a cloak. I leaned my head against the back of the chair, I was tired. She stood up to wipe my eyes and put her hands on my temples.

It was late now. The playing children were on their way home, the swans had gone into hiding, the flowers were gray. We went back down to the Saint-Jean center. Sabrya held my right hand until we got to my room. She helped the others put me to bed. She stayed for a few minutes, sitting on the edge of my bed, her hand on my cheek. I thanked her for everything she'd given me. She said she would telephone me; we would have lunch together on Monday. She kissed me on the forehead, closed my eyes. I barely heard her leave. I kept my eyes closed all night but couldn't sleep.

I kept my hopes up in the dark. I waited for the first rays of sunshine, then asked to be moved to the window so they could warm up my tired body. I drifted off into a dream. Sabrya was lying naked next to me. Our bodies were facing in the same direction. She curled up in the fetal position. I imagined the softness of her legs, I imagined my head close to hers, her hair spread on the pillow, the delicate nape of her neck. I fell asleep surrounded by her scent, by that dream.

She would live with me for all our remaining years. We would have lots of children. It would last until the end of time. She would talk to my children, laugh with Laetitia and Robert-Jean would be a little in love with her.

I dreamed of her being happy with this curious character from another world.

I shut my eyes in the sun. In the orange light behind my eyelids, I saw her with me, not as my girlfriend, but as a companion whom I would be entitled to kiss behind the ear as I whispered my sun-warmed dreams to her.

Obviously, she'd have to love me. But you couldn't do anything about that: it either happened or it didn't. Maybe it never would.

Horizon

I'D BEEN IN bed for three days, burning up. Three days of thunderstorms in Paris, and it felt as if all the water in the world couldn't bring me any relief. I just had to wait. Abdel would put a washcloth on my forehead and eyes to cool them down, or sometimes a folded sponge soaked in cold water on my neck, where I could feel the blood pulsing through the artery. That pulse would be the tempo of my waiting.

I stayed awake all Saturday night, the car headlights tracking across the ceiling gave the hours their rhythm. At one point a big fly appeared to distract me. It felt as if the atmosphere had changed, as if time had entered a new phase. I would have loved to be distracted by other flies, but there was only a before and after this one. Flies don't buzz around these days, bumping into windows, stopping in a corner somewhere for a few seconds, and then burbling off again. This one only made a single flight; I waited desperately for it to come back.

The darkness drew in, the contours of everything grew

blurred, my body floated on the humming, undulating bed. Every part of that endless expanse seemed to be on fire. I remembered the softness of Béatrice's body, the sheets. I shut my red eyes, a lump in my throat, as my spasms knocked the bed off its rhythm. I couldn't cry myself into a stupor, I had no tears left. I sensed the metal rod in my neck connecting my shipwrecked, unbearable body to my head, and all I could think was that I didn't want to sleep anymore; I didn't want to keep going over the past and coming up with images that would imprint themselves behind my eyelids. They were always of Béatrice. I turned my head to where she should have been. My ears rang in the silence; I felt my heart beat. I couldn't sleep, couldn't get any relief. I went over the last seconds of my crash, I should have . . . No, I had to concentrate on the children. The rest was hope, too painful. I just had to hold on. Not fall asleep forever. Wait for the morning nurse.

Abdel woke me up at one o'clock in the afternoon on Sunday. He thought I'd stopped breathing. A friend I hadn't seen for twenty years was coming to lunch. What did it matter if it was twenty years or yesterday, I still had to wait.

The Vietcong buried my uncle François, a missionary in Vietnam, alive. They just left his head sticking out of the ground, and tortured him to death. He was paralyzed like me, but the mass of earth kept him cool. It was his head that was on fire. He escaped through prayer. I waited for the sky to fall on me.

My friend arrived, another in a line of people who had

dropped in over the past three days or tried to ring but got no answer. After filling me in on the last twenty years of his life, without me uttering a word, he left. He didn't really know what to say. Sometimes a few days of his life would take him an eternity to describe, and then he'd make a year disappear in a few seconds.

The forces of gravity kept me solemnly pinned to the bottom of my bed.

Marc, my faithful physio, paid a visit as well. I didn't pay any attention to the exercises he made my lifeless body perform. He tried to make me laugh.

Alain de Polignac, my friend the prince, told me all the news from Champagne. I forgot it immediately.

Abdel lit a cigarette for me. The burning in my lungs was exquisite. I felt a chill rush through me like when I used to swim in the Vizzavona stream above Ajaccio as a child, or later, naked, with Béatrice. The burning sensation and the cold merged into one.

I waited for the dark.

AS THE days and weeks had passed, I had lost track of my memories; the past had become flattened and inert like me. The spirited, unstoppable, ambitious, hungry person I used to be no longer desired anything. It was all my fault. I'd killed her. I'd messed up my children. The future would only be worse. No woman would ever want to take me in her arms again. I was ugly, she'd gone. Why didn't they just pull the plug? I didn't want to be asked any more questions, I didn't have the strength anymore.

My body didn't react. Temperature: 93.2; blood pressure: 6. I raised my head, then passed out. Occasionally, the nurses tried to give me a shower. Then I'd sink down into the darkness. I'd lost all desire to go anywhere.

I was lying in bed. The allergies were making my face itch. I was listening to the *Goldberg Variations* too loud on my hi-fi.

Maybe I wanted to finish telling my story because a woman actually was here with me and I'd caught my second wind. Her presence was bringing me back to the world of people.

I had to go to the hospital. I felt freezing the minute I woke up.

Songs of Good Fortune

THE CAT WE called F-sharp died of feline AIDS; he had gone flat. Like me, in the past few days he had stopped eating. He wasn't strong enough to climb onto my bed anymore. I would look at him through the glass pane in my bedroom door, huddled in the hallway. He would meow in a strange way without even raising his head and refuse the tuna put in front of him. Laetitia told me he should go to the vet; I was stunned. Abdel offered to take him. The vet called me, "It's probably a virus, but we need to check some glands." Abdel brought him home; he spent his last night with me. The next day, his sentence was pronounced. And that's the last I heard about F-sharp, my faithful companion through all my nights of insomnia.

I loved and hated my loneliness. When the time came I'd go off into the darkness with a light heart, excited by the prospect of sharing the coolness of her grave. Mop my brow, stay with me tonight, I want to hear you breathe. Yesterday a baby had its afternoon nap next to me. I talked to it. I was thirsty. It would get worse later. All that smiling, all that charming people demanded; a wall of tears. The silence was white, incandescent.

I was haunted by loneliness. That's what made my future hardest to see. Locked in paralysis, in physical and emotional pain, kept at a distance by the look in other people's eyes. How was I going to survive when my children left (even if, in my dreams, I would be a permanent fixture in their everyday lives)? I already longed to be sent to a special facility to be treated for pain, however harmful it may have been to the reserves of lucidity that I still had. What would it be like in a few years, when a new layer of loneliness would have settled in, when my physical condition could only get worse? I had to be allowed a future, Sabrya couldn't always just be a dream.

*

IMAGINE HE is right. Imagine that the dead are resurrected on the eve of the Great Supper of God. It can't be just any reincarnation, mind you. It has to be a genuine resurrection of the body, just as Christ rose with His human body, with actual wounds that Thomas could touch. I don't want any messing around though. You're not going to resurrect me with my paralyzed body. No, I'm going to be transfigured like You. Even Mary Magdalene took a while to recognize You

He was handsome and luminous when He was resurrected. And so am I, as handsome as in the photo in Laetitia's room, in which I'm wearing an open, collarless, sky-blue shirt and standing against a backdrop of mimosas by Lake Geneva in Indiana. We had a small wooden house there.

They've left me for three days on the same daybed on which they had left Béatrice. My hair short as usual, I'm dressed in my charcoal gray suit, a white shirt with a tab collar, Grandpapa's gray-and-white checkered tie, and the black pocket handkerchief with Christian Lacroix in white letters. It's annoying that they've covered me with a tartan rug: it clashes with my suit, makes me look paralyzed, and I'm not cold anyway. When Christ appeared to the apostles, they were surprised because he didn't enter through the door or the window. That's the advantage of our transfigured bodies. Lying here comfortably without paralysis or pain, I can move but no one sees that. I even have a discreet fit of hysterics when an august relative catches his cane in the drawing room carpet and breaks his fall on the daybed. Someone lets out a scream of alarm. Only Béatrice in Heaven and the children hear me laughing.

At one point, I don't know the time, Laetitia and Robert-Jean want us to be alone together. They see me smile, which we keep as our secret, so now they know that I am going to be with Béatrice, that we're not going to suffer, and that we will watch over them with a boundless love. Children, we love you now as we have always loved you and always will.

I watch them all file past, sometimes with an ache in my heart. Sabrya is a mirage; Papa a vision of loyalty; Mama, of tenderness; Granny, of respect. Aunt Éliane is wearing her beautiful sky-blue suit, which goes so well with her eyes, tearstained though they are today.

During the service, Nicolas and Sophie sing the same pieces they sang for Béatrice. The pansies from my friend are on my coffin, pale blue this time, and the floor is a bed of white flowers.

My fragile mother-in-law leans on her daughter Anne-Marie's and son-in-law Jean-François's arms as she climbs up to the Dangu cemetery. I am overjoyed to see myself surrounded by all these children. The undertakers lower the slab with its mosaic of yellow chrysanthemums and purple irises over me. It rests on four points so Béatrice and I won't be shut in. It isn't necessary, but still, it is a nice thought.

"Hello, you crazy thing. Are you there, La Pozzo? Pozzolette, it's me! Béa sweetheart, Béatrice darling, it's me!"

No answer. The sounds of the living fade away.

"Say something, I can't stay here in this darkness all on my own."

A light appears through the shadows; Béatrice is more beautiful than ever.

"Look, I'm crying because I've found you again. I've missed you so badly, you shouldn't have left me those pages of despair. Sabrya . . . Is that what you're asking? Yes, she was beautiful and tender. She was the phoenix rising out of our love on earth, but that time is over now forever. I am ashes now, I have the passion of the risen to share. Shall we start right away? No, I have so many things to tell you. You know them already? Ah yes, that's true. Well, let's go for a walk under the stars, let's melt into each other as we stroll along. Wait, stop. I want to make up for the kisses I've missed. You know the children are well, don't you?"

Eternity . . . in your embrace.

Part Five

The Guardian Devil

Pater Noster

Our Father who art in Heaven
Stay there
And we will stay on earth
Which is sometimes so pretty

—JACQUES PRÉVERT,
"PATER NOSTER"

A BAD CHEST INFECTION had been cutting off the flow of oxygen to my brain. In the end I switched channels for a while, which, predictably enough, meant I was completely delirious when my synapses started up again. After a quick detour by way of paradise, I came around to find myself in a hospital bed—in Garches, I think.

"Oh! Coming back to earth now, are we?" Abdel said. "You've been ranting for five days. After a while it wasn't even funny anymore, you were on a different planet. You and these two women on either side of you, it's a nuthouse in here."

My neighbors, whose combined ages represented almost

two centuries of human existence, were quick to signal their presence by having a huge row. One of them—the meaner of the two—was confined to her bed; the other behaved like a little girl and kept coming to ask me for help. She wasn't all there, so couldn't grasp the fact that I was unable to move.

"Do you think she's going to go on making fun of me like this for long?" I grumbled.

She told me walking was a problem for her. "I get so tired!"

"Everyone has their cross to bear," I said.

After a while I could sit in my wheelchair and get a look at the other woman. It was hard to see her clearly, since there were bars around her bed to prevent her from making a murderous lunge for her neighbor. Part of her skull had been smashed in, so it seemed as if she hardly had a face under what was still a thick head of hair. She would lie on her side, staring fixedly at the door, talking in a language that no one recognized. My neighbor said it was the devil's. Her hoarse, strained voice was inhuman enough as it was; lying here naked in her bed, she infected everything with her madness.

I tried to explain to my neighbor that it was wrong to demonize her, that there had to be a suffering individual behind all that incomprehensible aggression. But I was wasting my breath. All the hospital staff came down hard on her. She was feral, answering the call of nature with such screams of fury that it would take an hour to clean up her room. So yes, she was crazy. Or, at any rate, very lonely.

My neighbor, who was at least ninety, repeated constantly, "I'm sick of it. It's so hard walking. I'm dead on my feet. What am I going to do now, sir? Come and have a look, sir . . . Come here for a couple of minutes, just a couple of minutes, come on, please, come here. . . ."

She still hadn't realized I was paralyzed. I called for Abdel, who sent her away. Now and then she'd stroke his face, seem to start crying, and go back to her room saying, "What is going to happen to me?" She would revert to a defenseless little girl again. I didn't understand how old people could just be abandoned like that.

Abdel, get me out of here!

*

I WASN'T going to give in though, this time or any other. I'd been a quadriplegic for more than eighteen years. A documentary had been made about my and Abdel's relationship, then a successful feature film, *Intouchables*. I had remarried, had two children with my wife Khadija, and moved to Morocco. I hadn't given up, which perhaps entitled me to a place in the pantheon of quads, not that I deserved any of the credit myself. I had kept going because:

→ I was lucky and rich enough not to have to be put in an institution. I don't know how anyone can survive when they're surrounded day and night by the despair of other equally disabled individuals, when they have

to hear them sob and scream, and watch impassively
as a room is sterilized.

+ The pain kept me angry. I couldn't doze off while I
was in such discomfort.

+ There was always a remarkable woman with me.
Béatrice, whom I left on the immutable boat heading
upriver, companions such as Clara, and finally
Khadija.

+ The children: my eldest, Laetitia; Robert-Jean; Sabah,
"the dawn"; and our youngest, Wijdane, "deep soul."

+ Abdel, ferryman between the riverbank and the
seashore.

Plus I loved the taste of coffee every morning at breakfast.

FOR MY sixtieth birthday, Khadija organized a surprise party
at our house in Essaouira. She choreographed it so that I arrived from Marrakech after the hundred or so guests, who
included my children; my mother; Aunt Éliane; my mother-
in-law, Lalla Fatima, and her family; my sister-in-law, Anne-
Marie; the Corsican family; friends from France and Morocco;
Yves and Max, my paragliding cronies; Abdel; and Eric and
Olivier, the directors of *Intouchables*.

Exhausted from the trip and the waves of emotion, I ad-
libbed a short speech thanking everyone for being there and
complimented a pianist friend of ours, who had given a wonderful performance.

"My darling wife. First let us remember the people who have left us: my dear mother-in-law who followed her daughter Béatrice with such bravery; Granny; and my father the duke, who passed away after meeting his last granddaughter, Wijdane. . . .

"Sixty years old! I had forgotten. In stocktaking, you tend to keep vegetables and meat separate—one of Abdel's jokes. I have been alive forty-two able-bodied and eighteen disabled years, which, like dog years, are worth seven of the other sort. I'll let you do the math.

"I would like to thank Abdel who has helped me from the moment I came out of the hospital twenty years ago. Extremely supportive when Béatrice died, he kept me and my children company through the hard years, saved my life on a number of occasions, and finally set me down in Morocco, where I was able to open my eyes and see Khadija. Now I know what happiness tastes like again."

Abdel was the guardian devil who put his wild years behind him to become my unlikely caregiver. Antagonistic to everyone, rebelling against everything, this desperado was now married with three children. He had become a chicken farmer, an *"éleveur de poulets,"* and since *"poulets"* was French slang for "the police," who had kept him on the run for so much of his life, he took a perverse pleasure in keeping them under lock and key.

The Bad Boy

CLAIMING TO BE all of five feet six, Abdel was a force of nature, a scaled-down version of Cassius Clay—or rather Muhammad Ali, as he'd correct me. His hammerlike fists could shatter a person's skull, not to mention inflict fractures to the jaw and elsewhere. His opponents would crumple to their knees before they'd even seen the blow coming. Abdel would just turn a little pale, although not for long—his usual smile would soon be back in place.

An absolutely square face and large jaw, he tore meat to pieces, wolfing down sixty pounds of mutton a sitting, a real grinding machine. A determined chin and small, bright, smiling eyes, which were always on the move. Shaved head, shaved face, always well-groomed and stylishly dressed in designer clothes.

Abdel didn't talk about his delinquent past much, but over the years I found out certain things about his stormy adolescence. I noticed he could run a blistering hundred-yard dash, for instance, so I told him once that he should have kept up with athletics.

"No need these days."

"Because . . . ?"

"Being a fast runner is only handy when you've got the cops on your tail."

I looked blank.

"Totally! You're never more than a hundred yards from the underground, and you're fine once you're down there."

"That didn't stop you getting caught though, did it?"

A few years after I had employed him, he had confessed to having been in prison.

"I was only in for a few months," he said.

"That wasn't very clever. What did you do?"

"Oh, just a little jewelry shop. The whole crew got nabbed."

I would get to know "the crew" when Abdel employed them for our rental car company. At least their knowledge of the police was something we didn't have to worry about.

Gleefully provocative, whenever he was with my aristocratic friends, Abdel would leap at the chance to make remarks along the lines of "The thing about prisons in winter, you see, is that they've got central heating. They're very comfy and you've got TV, haven't you?" His favorite subject when we had company, though, was the French social system. "Why do you expect me to go to work? I'm on income support, I get subsidized housing, free health care. . . . No, honestly, France is a good place," he said. "That can't change."

I could see from the faces of my guests that he was doing a sterling job recruiting for the National Front. He liked to play up his dodgy, petty criminal side. In fact, some of my friends were secretly concerned about my being around such a character. "Things falling off the back of a truck is my big specialty. What you do is you get a stolen truck, divide up the goods among your crew, and sell it on super quick. Sorry, we do not accept checks!"

I suspected this was something he still did. I was offered untold designer scents, telephones, laptops, stereos, televisions—the list went on.

"Abdel, you know I can't accept this sort of thing."

"No, look, it's quality, I'm telling you."

For my birthday, he gave me a huge jukebox containing two hundred CDs neatly done up in wrapping paper. I could listen to the classical music I loved for four days nonstop. He mischievously handed me the receipt, saying, "In case you have any problems with the warranty."

"Abdel," I asked him once, "aren't you tired of always being on the wrong side of the law? You hang around with pimps, fences, drug dealers. . . ."

"Careful!" he interrupted. "I don't do hookers or drugs. It's against my religion."

He didn't drink, he didn't smoke, but he was fairly broad-minded in all other respects.

He confessed to Mathieu Vadepied—the artistic director of *Intouchables,* who also made a documentary about us and the actors in that film—that he had served eighteen months for theft. Slightly more serious than "a little jewelry shop"!

Once, during one of my spells in bed, I was dictating a letter to my female assistant, Laurence, when two police officers appeared in my room: "We would like to ask you some questions about an individual who was caught on speed camera last night. According to our records, the vehicle is registered in your name."

"But of course, officer."

He handed me a photo of Abdel in one of my pretty cars.

"Oh yes, I recognize the car. Laurence, will you look in the courtyard to see if the blue Jaguar is there?"

Laurence—who understood the game—answered, "No, sir, your car isn't there."

"What, that can't be. Has it been stolen?"

"I don't know what to say."

"Do you know this individual?"

"No. Do you have any idea what he's called? What about you, Laurence?"

Laurence bent over the photo with an innocent expression. "No, sir, I really don't."

The officers weren't taken in. But, faced with a quad obviously in pain and struggling for breath, an immaculately dressed secretary in a miniskirt, and that setting, they thought it better to make themselves scarce. "Well, if you hear anything about your car or that individual, don't hesitate to call us."

"Absolutely, gentlemen. Thank you for coming."

Abdel cried with laughter when I told him.

"I got flashed by the river doing over ninety-five."

"Bravo, Abdel. What about the car?"

"This is all that's left of it," he said, handing me the keys. "It hit a wall."

He grimaced in pain; he'd fractured his pelvis and would need two hip prostheses, but he was still standing.

Abdel told the car story in January 2002 on Mireille Dumas's talk show, *Vie privée, vie publique*. Flabbergasted, she exclaimed, "Tell me this isn't true!" Shamefacedly, I confirmed that it was. Abdel then dug an even deeper hole for us. "It wasn't the only one either."

Such ostentation was a bit out of place given the day-to-day hardships experienced by most people with disabilities. Abdel and nuances!

Abdel and cars, meanwhile, would make a book in itself. He was constantly speeding, going the wrong way down one-way streets, driving too close to the car in front, ignoring traffic lights, closing his eyes, and so on and so forth. He dubbed himself "Ayrton Abdel."

One day, we were on our way to Dangu to check on the renovation work I was having done to an eighteenth-century wing of the château. Abdel was the self-appointed site manager. The Rolls-Royce was burning down the highway at nearly a hundred and twenty-five miles an hour.

"She can do better, my foot's not on the floor."

"Abdel, don't drive so close to the cars in front and keep your eyes open, please."

"Shit, there are cops at the toll. . . . Shall we do the 9-1-1 routine?" he asked, already reclining my electronic seat.

The policeman signaled for Abdel to pull over. I shut my eyes and went into my act.

"You were going a hundred and thirty."

"It's an emergency. His blood pressure is critical."

I gave a groan from my side of the car. Abdel lifted my hand, then let it flop back down onto the seat to emphasize my paralysis.

"If we don't unblock his piping any minute," he said, waving my disability card, "his head's going to explode!" The policeman hesitated, went off to consult with his colleague. Both then came back on their motorbikes, lights flashing, and cleared the way for us at top speed to the hospital in Vernon. "Brilliant!" Abdel roared, ecstatic. At the hospital, one of the bikers alerted the paramedics, while Abdel became a blur of activity, putting the pressure sore cushions on the stretcher and extracting me from the car as the police looked on in amazement. He asked for a pillow to put under my head. "He needs a subpubic catheter. It's a bladder outlet obstruction," he asserted, slapping me repeatedly about the face to get the blood flowing. He didn't even respond when the police withdrew, saluting.

"No need to go overboard," I muttered. Then I asked in a louder voice, "What happened, Abdel? My head hurts."

"Oh, have you come to, Mr. Pozzo? It's nothing, everybody, it must have unblocked by itself when we moved him."

Turning to the paramedic, he asked, "Could you open the door?" and slid me back into the car.

For the record, we did go on to visit the construction site set up by Abdel's so-called team of builders in our beautiful eighteenth-century stables. The period woodwork had been sawed up and used as fuel for a barbecue in the period fireplace. The newly installed windows weren't watertight and had already started warping. An able-bodied person wasn't able to get to the first floor without banging his or her head on the stairs.

"It won't be a problem for you and there's always an extra wheelchair for everyone else," Abdel commented airily.

The kitchen wasn't accessible from the dining room, so you had to go outside. The door to my shower room had been fitted backward so a wheelchair couldn't get through it. The list went on. I shut them down immediately.

On the way back, just for a change, I drew Abdel's attention to the fact that he was asleep and far too close to the car in front.

"Don't worry," he said, and then, for the umpteenth time on that road, bumped into the car in front as it slowed down.

I understood Mireille Dumas's incredulous expression.

The Capuchins of Rivière-du-Loup

EVERYTHING HAD GROUND to a halt. The Parisian winter stretched painfully ahead. My face was swollen from allergies; my heart was in my boots; I didn't get out of bed, the curtains were permanently drawn. No plans, no visits: the only thing that made any impression on my inert mind was music. Richard Strauss's last four lieder played on a continuous loop, filling the room with their celestial sound. Abdel put out the word to my cousin Antoine, who was always on call in a crisis. I was crying a lot, I'm sure, and not saying anything beyond "Not good," through gritted teeth when people asked me how I was. Abdel draped a damp towel over me and put a bag of ice on my head. I felt I was disappearing.

Antoine consulted my friends and suggested a retreat at the mouth of the Saint Lawrence River, in a small monastery run by Capuchin Sisters near Rivière-du-Loup.

"In a fortnight of agape therapy, Greek for 'love therapy,'" my cousin quoted from the brochure, to Abdel's obvious delight, "the individual will find release, whatever the wounds or errors of his or her past, in a peaceful, discreet, mutually supportive atmosphere." Abdel was already rubbing his hands together in excitement.

"Let's keep it above the belt please, Abdel."

"Oh yes," he enthused. "The Capuchins get our vote."

I informed the Sisters that I would be traveling with a heathen, whose presence would be indispensable for my stay.

A Canadian evangelical television channel had invited me to speak at its tenth anniversary celebrations. They had already interviewed me in Paris and the resulting program, which didn't put forward a particularly Catholic message, had been aired several times in Canada; apparently the outspoken, aristocratic quad in his beautiful town house went down well. I got in touch to confirm I would appear on their show, which coincided with the end of our retreat at the monastery.

Abdel asked for three in-flight meals on the plane.

He was in charge of hiring a car when we arrived in Montreal and came back with the biggest thing he could find, a Lincoln Continental limousine with tinted windows. It was snowing in Montreal, where we were due to spend the night. He suggested we have something to eat on the main drag of what passed for the city's red-light district. Finding a Kentucky Fried Chicken, he stuffed himself with their specialty while ogling the fine chickadees parading up and down the sidewalk. I told him he couldn't bring anyone back to the hotel. Offended, he said he had never had to pay to provide a service.

We set off the next day at dawn to drive more than six hundred miles at a snail's pace. He set the cruise control and dozed the length of the interminable highway until we eventually found ourselves on a small, snow-covered road running alongside the Saint Lawrence. It was dark and Abdel, who couldn't understand the locals' directions, was lost. Finally, in the middle of nowhere, we came across a long, wooden building perched above the river. We parked and an old Capuchin nun, whose order required a vow of poverty and chastity (Abdel's face was a sight), came out in the snow in her habit and sandals to greet us. A few other, more modest cars were already parked in the lot. The nun seemed surprised as much by our barouche as by its occupants. Abdel unfolded my wheelchair and yanked me out of my seat. I promptly went into spasms, sending the good woman into a momentary panic. The mother superior had never had dealings with pilgrims of our order before. She ran through the strict house rules: silence, one floor reserved for women (quick look from Abdel), the schedule. There was a sign above the door to Abdel's room saying, God Lives Here. "I should hope so" was his comment. It was not a very auspicious beginning.

The daily routine was spartan: up at seven (I was awake from five thirty anyway), lights out at ten thirty. Abdel was bored. It was isolated and the heavy snow and thick fog all the time we were there made driving difficult. He also didn't dare stray too far in case I blacked out, which I did several times. So he spent the day hanging around, and the night chasing girls. Prohibitions and locked doors were not going to be a match for him.

There were around fifty "patients," if that was the right name for us. At our first meeting I realized that these men and women of all ages were life's war wounded. Behind a facade of normality, they had been carrying around traumatic experiences for years, usually since early childhood: incest, abuse (sometimes by their parish priest), rape. I saw old people break down in tears; it had taken them more than fifty years to acknowledge their suffering. It was wonderful how compassionate everyone was, as they struggled with the burden of their secrets. All of us had been persecuted in one way or another, so it only required one person to speak up for everyone else to pour their hearts out. I understood why there were dozens of boxes of Kleenex dotted around the hall. Our sessions would have been manna from Heaven for a shrink.

Rigid in my uncomfortable chair, draped in the white sheet that Abdel had seen fit to deck me out in (he admitted to me that he'd been inspired by the shroud in a picture of the entombment of Christ in his room), I was the only person not to cry over my lot. The loss and pain I felt were a walk in the park compared to the horrors that were being expressed all around me. Intimidated by my paralysis, the white sheet, my silence, the others didn't dare approach me at first. But gradually they started to come over, especially the women, to confide in me. I was available, everyone knew where to find me, I had plenty of time, and I listened. Occasionally I'd also say a word or two to reopen the floodgates and listen while my interlocutor released another cathartic rush of emotion. I was the prone psychoanalyst, and the able-bodied patient would bend down toward me and open her heart.

At meals, which were theoretically conducted in silence and lasted an hour, our table was in great demand as a meeting place for the women whom Abdel saw at night and I listened to. We were summoned by the mother superior and asked to observe the contemplation rule. To no avail. There would be at least ten people in my room at rest times, and everyone laughing instead of praying. In the end the Sisters simply gave up and wrote off the whole retreat.

Abdel seemed to have an invigorating effect on the pretty, depressed women he met, and I am still in touch with many of them today.

That fortnight reinvigorated me.

On our way back, we stopped at a huge ice hockey stadium where the evangelical television channel was holding its anniversary celebrations. The audience of the faithful—although not the meek—was over five thousand strong. They whooped and hollered their approval, and burst into strident whistles if a speaker bored them. I listened to a former hockey champion still reeling from a revelation, and a pop singer dying of cancer who went over like a storm. A boxing ring had been set up in the middle of the arena. I told Abdel to turn my chair around every five minutes: despite the banks of cameras and big screens, I wanted to be sure I addressed everyone there.

The owner of the pious channel and his boyfriend, whom we had entertained in Paris, announced us with an elaborate fanfare, giving my title and all the rest of it. Abdel put the Adonis in charge of getting my wheelchair into the ring, which proved to be quite a lot to ask of him, and then Abdel grabbed me in his arms and swung me over the ropes. The rowdy, massive audience fell silent. I hadn't prepared anything.

"I want to talk to my fellow wheelchair users, to everyone with a disability of any sort—in other words I want to talk to all of you, because we are all handicapped by life. . . ."

Prolonged applause, the audience was on their feet (except the guys in wheelchairs of course). I told them about the privileged child I had been, about Béatrice, about the lessons life had taught me. I said I preferred the riches that paralysis had brought me to those of my class: I felt I was living more intensely, that at last I was human.

Abdel had timed and choreographed everything; we were treated to a five-minute standing ovation as I left the ring. A mass of wheelchairs had moved down to the exit aisle to speak to me. I spent an eternity trying to kiss a pretty quadriplegic; her tearstained eyes said everything that needed to be said. We thanked the organizers and made our getaway, exhausted, before catching the plane home.

Hope, That Little Slip of a Girl

I DIDN'T COME BACK from Canada possessing any stronger faith, but I was convinced that everybody, whether they believe in God or not, craves hope. The question of God's existence didn't obsess me. I derived no pleasure from thinking about it and I didn't have the requisite emotional or spiritual constitution. But if solidarity and fraternity born of a common condition inspired me to belong to a community—of the disabled or of the religious—and observe its rituals, why should I object?

Whereas Béatrice had faith in eternity, I found hope in our miseries, in the little day-to-day things that may contain a seed of something better. Rejoice, all ye with disabilities, for hope comes naturally to you!

As Charles Péguy wrote in *The Portico of the Mystery of the Second Virtue*:

"But hope, said God, that does surprise me.

Even me.

That is surprising.

That these poor children see all that happens, and they
believe that tomorrow will be better . . .

But it is hoping that is difficult. (In a low voice shamefacedly.)

And the easy way, and the inclination, is toward despair
and that is the great temptation."[2]

How many friends in chairs had I lost to despair? A world
without hope was hell.

In his devastating poem, "All Souls' Day, 1836," the Spanish writer Mariano José de Larra envisioned looking into
his heart and finding only despair. "Holy Heaven! Another
graveyard? My heart is nothing but another sepulcher! Who
lies dead here? Frightful epitaph! 'Here lies hope.' Silence, silence." A year later, he committed suicide at age twenty-six.

It was up to us to combine Jean-Paul Sartre's useless passions with perseverance, the fruit of hope.

*

FRIENDS OF Béatrice's had set up a group to read the scrip-
tures and pray with her. We continued after her death. The
Bible is no picnic, it has to be said. Pain and suffering greet

---

2   Charles Péguy, *The Portico of the Mystery of the Second Virtue*, trans. Doro-
thy Brown Aspinwall, Scarecrow Press, 1970.

one on every page. Sickness, children dying, infertility, persecution by enemies, humiliation in all its forms, loneliness, the desertion and ingratitude of friends, the infidelity of lovers, scandal, the flourishing of the wicked, murders, wars—all this is the bedrock of existence. The book of Revelation seems more real than life itself.

A friend of mine, who had just inherited a staggering fortune, was asking me about the compatibility of wealth and Christian morality. "Listen," Abdel interrupted him, "if you don't know, don't worry, I'll know what to do with it."

"What about you, Abdel, do you believe in God?"

"Yes, but I don't practice, I haven't got the time these days. I practice in practical ways. I keep the faith, observe my customs, my traditions. Religion is the foundation of our moral values," he said, covering a lot of ground. "I don't like people who only think about God when they need something from Him. Religion does not stop me from doing anything. . . . Religion has never forbidden anyone to do anything. People often hide behind it to get out of doing what they should."

Amen!

The Bringers of Consolation

*C*ONSOLARE, THE LATIN verb from which "to console" is derived, means "to keep whole." I owe the fact that I am still in one piece unequivocally to women.

Abdel liked chubby women. After having a go, he would offer them to me with comments and notes.

"Not my cup of tea, Abdel."

I knew what I was talking about, since I had sampled—through no choice of my own—a "present" from Abdel. Music filled my darkened room, like the neuralgia racking my body, when Abdel poked his head around the door and said, "I've got an aspirin for you." He stepped aside to allow a stranger to pass. "Goodnight . . ."

Her name was Aisha and she unceremoniously slipped out of her clothes and joined me in bed. She curled up on my shoulder. We couldn't have exchanged more than a couple of words. She was caring and didn't seem put off by my condition. Her presence was calming and in the end, I dozed off.

A sumptuous rider straddled me and brought me back to the stable a few months later, exhausted. An abandoned wife mothered me excessively, and for too long. One of my neighbors, a man of leisure, sent me a courtesan after reading the first installment of my memoirs. Abdel hid behind the door, giggling, as the "masseuse" worked on my ears, among other things.

Sessions with the daughter of a Malian princess and Swedish sailor punctuated my sleepless nights. She herself was surprised by my needs.

A tall, restless Valkyrie stormed in and offered me cocaine, which relaxed her to a spectacular degree. She caroused interminably, bobbing around like a drunken boat drifting in the current, until she curled up in a ball and fell asleep.

And then there was Clara. She had got to know Béatrice at Larmor-Plage when I was in the hospital in Brittany. She called me in Paris one day when I was in despair. She spent the night, then a fortnight, then two years on and off. Her innocence reminded me of everything I believed in before my soul lost its way. She made me forget my ill-mannered appetites. I talked to her constantly. She would concentrate completely, absorbing my words, and then interrupt me with a kiss. Her attention was intoxicating.

She was lonely, and my abandon won her over. She remembered the dreams she'd had as a teenager; the years of betrayal faded away; she began to hope again. She negotiated with the limitations of my condition. Her candor aroused me, and the openness of her response to my defeated body inspired a sad, peaceful feeling of gratitude. Soon her quiet breathing brought comfort and lent rhythm to my nights.

I would look at her in her royal-blue suit and lover's dreams would play at the edges of my exhaustion. I'd see her walking along the avenues in the park with me. She wouldn't know where to position herself around my body. I'd lift my head and stare at her; she would kiss me, her eyes closed.

At night the images moved to the beat of the blood pulsing in my neck. I would feel our quiet games. Lazily emerging desire slowed our bodies. She unfurled like a cloud. Her deliberate hand caressed her heavy breast. We met at some midpoint between her momentum and my watchful participation, her self-restraint such that she almost shared my paralysis, the wave imperceptible until a sigh registered in her eyes. Snuggled up by my side, her desires finally assuaged, her lips parted, she would smile at me so I wouldn't cry and murmur endearments. She accepted my spasms as a token of my passion. A new code for our love emerged from my uprooted body.

But when she was away, I didn't react. I would acknowledge my powerlessness to myself and start to wait again. I didn't nourish my inner life, my pointlessness irritated me.

Very well, I decided, I'd write to her.

*

Clara,

*I'm in bed. I dread your falling silent for good. I think
your beauty may be starting to mean something different to
me, which is less to do with desire than a sweet connection
between our scattered days. This is just the sort of peaceful
continuity I yearn for.*

*Let's invent a plausible future. You'd be lying next
to me, our bodies apart, impassive partner, impalpable
presence. When this minute gap became unbearable, you
would come and put your head on my neck, and perhaps
lay your body on my insensible flesh. You would close your
eyes on this cold embrace and lull yourself again with your
rueful senses.*

How can I ask you to embark on this tentative journey?

How sad the imagination is.

Refocus me. I will be compliant.

The Front Line of Acculturation

ABDEL DIDN'T WANT to be beholden to anyone for anything, whereas I was conciliatory by necessity; I was dependent on other people.

"Don't be high-handed," I'd say to him. "Not everything is black or white, Abdel. A sense of nuance is essential to understand life."

He loved getting a rise out of people. He told my brother, for instance, who is a computer scientist, that there was a mistake in a program he had written. Abdel couldn't even turn on a computer! My brother's reaction thrilled him, the troublemaker.

In front of an audience of people with disabilities, he singled out one particularly afflicted soul, whose body was intensely contorted, and said, "It is easier for someone with a disability to find a job than an Arab."

Stunned silence.

"Only kidding, of course!"

The whole room burst out laughing.

The key tenets of Abdelian philosophy: everything is screwed; death is inevitable; everything else is comedy. And, most important of all, do not participate in political activity of any kind. "It's a waste of time; they're all corrupt."

"What about young Muslims killing themselves for the sake of freedom and justice?"

"OK, but that means something different to them—in the world I live in, everyone steals, the housing projects are on fire, the old are left to die alone, sex is everywhere, it's everyone for himself. So I try to get the most out of everything, I do my thing and too bad if it pisses other people off."

He had a point.

"But Abdel," I continued, "you're a perfect example of the West. The philosophy of everyone for himself plays into the hands of the rich. The more you think just of yourself and ignore other people, the more vulnerable you are."

Perplexed looks from Abdel.

ABDEL WAS offended by the abstract art I collected.

"It's just a luxury for small-minded rich people. If I need an interpreter to explain a painting to me, that's because there's a problem with it."

At a Zao Wou-Ki exhibition, when I went into raptures

about his legacy, the traces of his influence in other people's work, he said, "I can leave some other traces if you like."

"Abdel, you're right. Almost all contemporary art is apolitical, art for art's sake. But there are some brilliant artists whom people rally around and are accessible, even to you, Abdel."

"Accessible? At those prices? I bet their bank managers think they're brilliant too. We don't see things the same way, you and me."

At one point I staged an exhibition in the town house of work by a young artist who'd been at the École Polytechnique and supposedly combined algorithms and art.

"I can do you the same for one zero less," Abdel said.

"I'm with you there, Abdel, but his girlfriend is very pretty, so that balances everything out."

"Expensive way to go about it."

WHEN WE met Abdel didn't listen to music. By the end he enjoyed Mozart and Bach. I put on a concert at home with the Psophos Quartet, four charming female musicians, who played Schubert's *Death and the Maiden*. Abdel woke up when it was over, saying, "That wasn't bad, very sixteenth century."

ONE SUBJECT we argued about was our view of women, whom Abdel belittled en masse.

"Women take away all your freedom, I can't stand it. They should just keep their mouths shut."

"Women deserve respect, Abdel."

"Respect? Let's put it this way: it's not up to us to respect them, they have to earn our respect. And look: there's raw materials, which I like, and then there's a work of art, isn't there? It's got to be romance with a capital "R" for you; nice bodywork is what matters to me."

"Abdel, women create the bonds between people."

"It's criminal to do that to a child," he said after a pause, almost to himself. I realized he was thinking about his childhood, the trauma of being sent away to live with his uncle, but before we could discuss it, he added authoritatively, "God can't be a woman. Can you imagine her having her period every month! What kind of impression would that make? It has to be a guy."

More than anything else, Abdel didn't want to become attached.

"One-night stands, that's all."

"Abdel, you will have to have children one day, and enter the stream of history."

It was only when he was at peace and confident about his place in society that Abdel would be able to start a family.

*

Clara,

Thank you for your beautiful, pointillist letter. How lucky you are to be able to dream about light and colors.

I don't have dreams anymore, just hopes. Often the words run into one another as I dictate until they're just sounds. I lie there with my eyes open, feeling Béatrice above me. Discordance.

Time flags, my body fades, phrases float like moats of dust in the light. The pianist lightly brushes his keys. I'm miles away, seeing those who are no longer with us. I have to come back, hold my head up even though everything makes me want to curl up in a ball. Finally I'm on the soothing horizontal, darkness sets in, there are people here. For how long?

It's so important for me to be able to see the few people who are precious to me like you, dear Clara. The memory of those brief moments stays with me when I am far away.

No Further Bets!

$M.$ POZZO, WHY don't we start a business?"

"In my condition? I am not really in the swing of things anymore. I don't know if I want to be either.'"

"I've got a friend who runs a garage, and he's making shitloads. You can charge people anything when they need their cars fixed."

"That's not business, Abdel, it's a scam. To do well in it, you need to have a new slant, and since neither of us is a mechanic, we'd need to think of a service we could offer."

"You see," Abdel smiled. "You've still got it."

At last, I had something concrete to think about during my insomniac nights. A distinctive, long-term venture that would suit me and be up Abdel's alley . . . His knowledge of mechanics didn't extend beyond the numerous car crashes he had been in. He had delivered pizzas for a year though. What about a car rental company where you dropped off the car at the customer's home?

Abdel loved it.

"Delivery wouldn't be a problem. You'd have to cover all of Paris, twenty-four hours a day, seven days a week. I've got just the guys for the job."

"Abdel, it'll have to be eight-hour shifts."

"No, my boys don't work like that."

I asked to meet the team: Yacine, twenty years old, a good-natured giant; Youssef, same age, a skinny black guy from the Algerian desert; Djebar, the oldest, who didn't speak; and finally, Alberto, a twenty-five-year-old Italian Moroccan. Not forgetting their three pit bulls.

"They look like maniacs," I commented after they'd left. "Where did you find them?"

"We've all done time together."

The team distributed ten thousand leaflets. Abdel—who had assumed the role of operations manager—barked orders at them left, right, and center. When I expressed reservations, he replied that that was how you managed employees in his country. They didn't seem to turn a hair either for that matter, no doubt because they were afraid of their boss's physical strength and his propensity to use it to get his point across.

We took out a wonderful half-page advertisement in *Le Parisien* and we were inundated with phone calls. Things got off to a flying start, and then took an equally speedy turn for the worse. Abdel's four minions were a disheveled lot when I met them. He hardly gave them any time to rest, so the problem became chronic. For his own part, he stopped shaving.

Laurence, my assistant whom I had seconded in the business, gave him an ultimatum. "Either your boys tidy up their mess before I get into the office in the morning, and their three pit bulls relieve themselves in the street rather than on my carpet, or you find someone else to work with you."

As I was being driven to the office for the first time, a car pulled out into the road in front of us from the right, boxing us in. Abdel shot out of his seat to hurl abuse at the guilty party. The fellow lowered his window and pointed out that he had the right-of-way. First mistake, which earned him a haymaker. The guy dived into the glove box and pulled out a huge knife. Second mistake. Yacine grabbed him by the collar and thrust him toward Abdel, who dealt him a tremendous blow. The man was left bleeding, slumped over the steering wheel.

"Are you sure all that was necessary?"

"It's the only way with idiots."

"You look a little off-color, M. Pozzo," Laurence said when I arrived. "I'm not sure you'll be able to take the office."

We were met by an unbearable smell and the pit bulls roaming around off the leash. Abdel barked an order and the three creatures lay down. A cubbyhole to the right was being used as a kitchen; dirty dishes were stacked in piles, mint tea was brewing away. The receptionist was talking on the telephone, a scarf clamped over her nose. The movers' boxes still hadn't been unpacked, files were scattered all over the floor.

"The furniture's coming tomorrow," Abdel said.

"It's been doing that for a fortnight," Laurence snapped.

What was supposed to be my office was the team's dormitory. There were blankets on the floor and garbage in the gaps between them. Emergency meeting! And soap for these gentlemen, please!

Laurence ran through the results: very high rates of use, equally high rates of complaint. A number of cars, she added, had ended up on the scrap heap.

I was tired and didn't feel like arguing. On the opposite curb, I spotted one of our Peugeot 605s with its hood smashed in.

"It's no problem," said Abdel. "The mechanic's going to sort it out for us with a claims adjuster he knows."

A girlfriend who had used our service called me to relate her experiences. A big hulk in jeans and sneakers had turned up almost an hour late; the car was filthy, there was no gas in the tank, plus he had the nerve to ask her to drop him in Paris.

On another occasion, Laurence told me she'd just spoken to the Lyon police. Abdel had been arrested with an accomplice. The police had discovered an injured passenger in his trunk. "The customer was three days late," explained Abdel. "My friends found him in Lyon and we've just got our car back."

It was evidently an acquaintance who had abused Abdel's trust in some way. Swollen-faced, the captive had cleared my operations manager of all wrongdoing to prevent further acts of retaliation. I saw Abdel that evening. Of course, he was overjoyed.

"Abdel, what the hell is this mess? We don't rent our cars out to crooks and gangsters, and please, when we have respectable customers, show them a little respect."

"You don't know how much I take that to heart. The day before yesterday, I had to personally satisfy a customer who was a bit on the large side."

I was appalled and worried.

After taking stock with Laurence, discovering that a third of the fleet was under repair and enduring her litany of complaints, I announced the closure of the company. The joke had lasted six months and hurt my bank accounts considerably.

In a somewhat foolhardy way, I suggested that Abdel think of something a bit more in his line of work. It didn't take him long to come back with a suggestion of his own: "You should buy tenant-occupied flats at auction. You can get some real bargains."

"Naturally. The rents are controlled."

"That's not a problem."

Abdel hauled me up to the auction house. The auctioneer and the bidders fell silent as we made our entrance. When the first apartment we were interested in came up, I nodded to indicate I was making a bid, as I did at Drouot when I was buying works of art. Seeing no reaction from the auctioneers, Abdel sprang from his seat, ranting and railing, and raised my arm, which sent me into spasms all over. "Look, he made a bid!" Everybody loved that.

We came back several days in a row and bought five

apartments in trendy neighborhoods. Abdel then "managed" them: in other words, he sent his minions to eject the tenants, did some rudimentary improvements, and then filled the vacancies.

The accounting was nonexistent, they made no money, and I sold them.

*

Clara,

Let all this confusion pass you by and use our truncated memories to model a simple, frugal version of me. Impose your boundaries on my scattered self, contain me with your actions, surround me with your intentions, reassemble me out of my remains. Disintegrated, colorless, and without substance, what do I have to offer you?

How I'd love to feel your hands on my forehead, your mouth bringing me back to life, even if only in part, making me strong and real.

Every day your letters give me back my freedom; I love rediscovering sensations through your words. This lifeless body of mine has barred me from the past, so let us identify the present, the moment. Let us add up our tomorrows and make a past, then we shall have a shared memory, a new horizon.

A Parturient World

CHRISTIAN VALUES—CONCERN FOR others, the contemplative life, frugality—have long been the values of the Western world; humanism is their heir. And yet the modern West of consumerism and the markets has forgotten them. They have taken refuge among the needy. Thus the Six Commandments of the Quad are:

→ DISABILITY estranges you from your body, not from other people. Seek them out.
→ Silence is liberating. Be quiet.
→ Pain only leaves time for the essential. Don't fritter away the time you have on the trivial.
→ You are not alone. Find consolation.
→ Paralysis engenders patience. Wait.
→ We are all so fragile. Live in a spirit of fraternity, solidarity, and simplicity.

The free-market West's only commandment, however, is: Me, me, and more me. Multisensualism—the cult of the body, the search for more comfort and sensation—shall prosper.

Everything in excess—orgies, frenzies, noise, oblivion.

My accident had shown me the barbarism of our complacent world: the misery of loneliness, the debilitating effects of unemployment, the lack of opportunities for young people, the relentless accumulation of wealth. I saw the growing radicalization of a financially driven system, and, in its wake, the global spread of a shortsighted concept of time, which was destroying societal and familial safeguards.

When I taught the ethics and management classes Abdel found so soporific, my argument, which seemed to go down well, ran:

> → RESPECTING the values that come naturally to people with disabilities produces better forms of wealth creation. On reflection, you will see these are your values too.
>
> → A single group cannot continually appropriate all the wealth. An increase in profits without an increase in redistribution kills demand: it is the ultimate instance of a society shooting itself in the foot. The social contract only works if both parties gain, if the fruits of the joint enterprise are shared, and if the nation's wealth is redirected to the needy.

→ Don't let financial interests divide and rule: form
parties, unions, associations . . . Respect the rigor of
numbers.

→ Obtain justice from the murky, lawless, faithless
powers that be, so you can assert what is real and
restore the rule of law.

→ Use new information technologies to contest what is
happening.

→ What's truly global is not capital but the organizations
people form.

O ye with disabilities, on your feet!

*

Clara,

*My soul doesn't delight in the beauty of the world
anymore. My flesh is rubble. I have got lost somewhere
between my first passions and today's neglect. I feel
indifferent to everything. Let's go back to the wellspring; I
know the waters will be cool with you at my side.*

*I am depending on you for these dreams. Lend them to
me and I will give you my changeable identity in return.
I long to start again, to do away with the dark times of
suffering and resignation. If you take the first step, we can
be open with each other from now on.*

Role Play

LET'S IMAGINE AN inverted world, where serenity is the norm and agitation the exception. On Sundays in this world, legions of wheelchairs mosey around the Bois de Boulogne zoo, the Jardin d'Acclimatation, and study the manic able-bodied figures in each of the cages. Children especially enjoy the fat hairy man who paces frantically around in circles, his hand crushing a pink phone against his crimson ear. He yells a litany of complaints at his little neighbor, who teeters on his heels. They both have a row of watches on each wrist and an undone tie spilling over their tracksuit tops. They don't even stop gesticulating when they take a piss. This is the children's favorite moment and they nod their heads in applause.

At the full moon, when these traumatized souls finally fall into their medicated sleeps, the tribe of the disabled rises and the promised land is theirs. This is the night they make love. Women's hips become supple again, men regain their erections. Neither so common that it could ever lose its delight, nor so rare that it could inspire despair—this is paradise.

Imagine not talking for a few hours: when you start again, you might hear something special in the words, a melody you didn't hear before. Go into a coma: when you wake up, you might find yourself beholding beauty.

Now try a short-term death: the real version should be welcome after you've gone through hell.

I find the absurd a relief. Tomorrow is my day of oblivion. Perhaps God will come and whisper in my ear that He exists. Béatrice, can you intercede on my behalf and ask Him to give me a full life, exempt from my condition? How unimportant, spending your whole life extricating yourself from your shackles! Let Him inspire all geniuses at birth. What stupid crosses we bear! History, let us go once and for all, won't you?

*

Clara,

Last night I had a burlesque dream. A gigantic woman with a few corkscrew twists of black hair and an obscene mouth was lying on her back in thick grass in the throes of labor. Out popped an imp. He could run the moment he was born, her little goblin, and a brutal smile crossed his baby face as he took to his heels. Recovering instantly, his mother set off after him, the ground shaking under her heavy tread. She drooled with desire for her offspring, her arms outstretched, howling

*my name, as the toddler chased after a little girl, his cock
already hard.*

*The scene broadened to show frenzied creatures of
every sort: some were stopping, legs splayed, to give birth;
others were fighting each other; others were making love.
Pursued by the restless moon, the earth revolved, languid-
eyed, around the sun, as a beautiful star blushed with
longing for its neighbor. At last I understood the universal
law of desire. A man's cock, a woman's breasts—the land
of milk and honey!*

*Oh, I'm so happy to be in a bawdy mood—don't be
angry with me. You've allowed me to feel there can be
such a thing as comedy again.*

The Generous Godfather

IT HAD BEEN raining in Paris for weeks, and I had been in bed—burning, abrasive, and discouraged by the silence.

"You know, the day after tomorrow is your godson's birthday—the Yankee," Abdel told me. "He's going to be eighteen. You've got to do something."

"Please take care of it, Abdel."

John was the son of good friends of Béatrice's and mine from Chicago. I was putting him up during his year abroad in Paris.

Abdel came back the next day to report that everything was organized and that he'd lined up a belly dancing show.

Slightly anxious, I reminded him, "Nothing in bad taste, Abdel."

"Don't worry."

On the evening of the party, he dressed me in my dinner jacket, black tie, white handkerchief. I was lying in my electric wheelchair so I wouldn't faint. The teenage guests my children had rounded up were dressed to the nines. Only the most fashionable of the fashionable, the bluest blood of all of France. The champagne flowed, the petits fours circulated, the sound system howled. I started sweating and thought I was going to pass out. Abdel lifted my legs above my head. The youths edged away uneasily.

With an effort, I pulled myself together and addressed the hundred or so guests. Abdel gave John his present: a digital camera. Applause.

"Now, if you could find somewhere to sit against the walls. Abdel has been kind enough to prepare a show for us."

Abdel put on some Eastern music. Like a high priest of the revels, he flung open the double doors to the next room. Nothing happened. He turned up the volume.

In stormed a magnificent creature, who was not a belly dancer, but was undeniably oriental and totally naked. Astonishment, cries of surprise from the assembled company; they sat, frozen, as the naiad made a tour of the room, undulating sinuously before a sea of bright red faces. John, who was sitting on my right, looked at me furiously. "This isn't your doing, is it, Uncle?"

The creature suddenly loomed in front of me, unfortunately leaving me cold; I didn't even feel the urge to laugh. She'd gathered I was the boss, and started swaying her hips back and forth. I let her know it was my neighbor's birthday. She sat on his lap, and he held out for thirty seconds before leaping up from his seat and shoving her off. This was the signal the others had been waiting for: they all started scream-ing. The boys fled into the chilly garden and the girls, slightly less riled, stayed in the warmth and chattered away.

"The party was very nice, Uncle," John told me when it was time to go out. "It was lucky my parents weren't here though. No need to send them any photos, I don't think."

He kissed me affectionately and rejoined his gang. Abdel took me back to my rooms. I passed the enchantress, swathed in a fur coat and escorted by her manager—a pimp if ever I saw one.

Abdel showed them out.

"Nice Mercedes those two have. What about her, what did you think of her bodywork?"

"Abdel, I thought I asked you for something tasteful."

"Well, she's not a pro."

"You can explain that to John. Anyway, thank you for your help. Can you put me to bed now?"

I asked him to play a Bach cello suite.

The next day, a friend, regally indifferent to what anyone else thought, was the only person to put in an appearance. "Such a pity we weren't invited!"

Herbaceous and Loquacious

Everything seemed worse the following evening. Abdel's "present" had shocked people and hadn't exactly gotten me back on my feet. He heard me groaning in my room and said into the intercom: "Not feeling good?"

I moaned despondently. He got me dressed and pushed me to Saint-Germain-des-Prés. He stopped outside chez Castel.

"Oh no, Abdel, not these assholes."

"It's nothing. I've just got to pick something up."

There were some flashily dressed drunks standing at the club entrance. Abdel went over and talked to a few of them, jerking his chin in my direction. One—a big lug who needed a shave—took out a packet of cigarettes, lit one, and handed it to him. Abdel came back with a big smile.

"Here, smoke this."

"Revolting, he can't even afford a normal cigarette," I muttered. Abdel pushed me to the Deux Magots, and by the time we were at a table, my head had started spinning.

"What is this stuff?"

"A little hash never hurt anyone."

"For goodness' sake, Abdel, I've never touched this shit. You could have asked me."

"Ah, it's starting to have an effect . . ."

"Abdel, you didn't do a good thing by John. You've got to respect young people. Women too."

"It was just a joke."

"It's not a joke being eighteen, boys are sensitive. You wouldn't have done that to your kid . . ."

I was on a roll. Abdel let it go.

"Fine," I continued, "all society cares about is fucking, but young people . . . I mean, they're not against it, but they believe in love. A woman is private, she's not some piece of merchandise you put on display. She's someone you respect, someone you think of sharing your life with. . . ."

"A life sentence. Yup, I'm with you there."

"When you have a family, you'll fight for them, you'll want to pass on the things you believe in, what you consider beautiful, Abdel. Not a nice pair of breasts, but the beauty of family, of real relationships, of growing up. . . ."

"Growing hard, you mean?"

"Generosity to those weaker than you, friends you can count on . . . Everything, in a word. You'll see, in a few years, you'll want to fight anyone who ogles your girl."

"Want to bet? Come on, put it there!"

"Very funny, Abdel . . . Ah, it's true, this stuff does make you feel good. We'll have to get some more."

"No problem."

I witnessed the delivery of a brick of pure resin: Abdel whistled out of the car window and a package was thrown down from a third-floor window. I'd turn to this "remedy" in stormy weather until I found myself under beautiful Moroccan skies, in its country of origin.

*

Clara,

I want you to respond to my scattered fragments, confront my nonexistence with your reality. Equip me with your breathing so that my drugged memory can sketch out a path to take. Perhaps you'll help me find the thread again. If only I could at least resume my odyssey.

Give me something to yearn for, please. Challenge me, help me. After Béatrice died, I gave up. If only I could discern the faint spark of a new life somewhere in this dark labyrinth of pain and feigned casualness. What will we find under the banked-up ash of this long night? Will it be the same troubled soul? Or will the fire catch again somewhere else, lighting up the days to come with its warm glow?

Morocco

LAETITIA ADVISED ME to seek out fairer climes in which to spend the six months of the year I found so grim in Paris. Abdel suggested Marrakech with its dry winters. He organized everything. When we arrived, a magnificent Mitsubishi was waiting for us, courtesy of one of his friends, the king of Moroccan chicken. The intended apartment, however, had disappeared.

"No problem, I've got an address."

We made our way across the main square, Jemaa el Fna. He bumped me over the cobblestones and, turning down a cul-de-sac, knocked on the door of an unmarked building. A blond welcomed us into her riad, one of those beautiful traditional Moroccan homes built around a courtyard. Her welcome was particularly effusive because she had seen us on television the night before, on a repeat of *À la vie, à la mort,* produced by Mireille Dumas. Abdel turned on the charm while I asked to lie down, exhausted from the trip. I was shown to a large room on the ground floor adorned with mashrabiya windows, which let in the cold. Abdel asked for heaters.

He went out to unpack the car. An hour later, he still hadn't come back.

"Abdel, where are you?" I asked him on the phone.

"It's nothing, just got a little problem to sort out. I'll be right there."

It was Abdel's standard response when he was in a fix. Half an hour later, there was still no sign of him.

"I'm with the cops," he told me over the telephone. "I'll be a few more minutes."

It was difficult to know what was going on.

"Do you want me to get involved?"

"No, no. No problem."

Just then, my usual pain started. After an eternity, he showed up—the little devil—in an extremely perky mood and with a bandage on his right hand.

"Abdel, what happened?"

"It was nothing. I just ran into some jerk-off parking attendant who called me a dirty Algerian. He didn't want to help, so he didn't get his tip."

Egged on by his friends, the attendant had laid hands on Abdel and received a violent uppercut for his pains. His face was covered in blood and several teeth had exploded out of his mouth.

"I caught one in my fist," Abdel said, laughing.

"Why did you take such a long time though?"

"Those bastards dragged me off to the station. I slipped the superintendent five hundred dirhams and now the other guy's in the can. I filed a complaint against him. He's going to be in for a fortnight."

I thought that sounded a bit harsh, but Abdel was in an unforgiving mood.

By way of goodnight, he said as he turned out the lights, "It should warm up in here in a few hours. I'll go and heat up the blonde in the meantime."

"Abdel, don't be stupid. She's with someone."

Throughout the night I was woken by furious panting and intermittent screams. After a while, there was silence. Then it all started again. It was not particularly restful.

"How did you sleep?" Abdel asked me in the morning.

"I had a restless night. Maybe a wretched one."

He beamed; he was having a great day.

"Mine was steamy!"

"Abdel! For goodness' sake, she wasn't on her own."

"Well, he shouldn't have fallen asleep then. The idiot."

"Do you realize what a racket you were making?"

I saw the woman soon afterward. She looked tired but she maintained her dignity. Abdel, the soul of innocence, remarked, "M. Pozzo, did you know our hostess is getting married next week?"

I had trouble keeping a straight face.

While waiting to find suitable accommodations, we decided to travel around the country. Crossing the snow-covered

Atlas Mountains was epic. "Abdel, when the road's icy, slow down before turns. And, if you start skidding, turn into it." He did exactly the opposite and we crashed into a wall of frozen snow, crumpling the fender and blocking the wheel. He straightened it with the jack and drove on in annoyed silence.

After Ouarzazate, we skirted the peaceful Draa valley. Abdel careered around in the dunes, and naturally got stuck in the sand. It took three camel drivers and their mounts to get us out. "Isn't this the best?" Abdel remarked.

We drove back to Fes—that superb, decrepit city—and then on to the Mediterranean, to Saidia and its huge beach on the Algerian border. Abdel checked us into the only hotel with central heating. There was a bar outside, which meant we'd hear brawling all night long. Abdel made sure he didn't miss out on the fun.

He gave the receptionist a big smile.

"Abdel, I see you haven't been idle," I remarked.

"No," he retorted indignantly, "it's not that sort of place!"

We had lunch in a straw hut on the beach. "In summer," he said, "almost two hundred thousand Moroccans come back here from abroad in their beautiful BMWs or Mercedes loaded with cash. All these cafés make unbelievable money then."

I could feel him counting his wad of notes.

We would have the opportunity to return to Saidia four times and meet its great Wali, the local representative of government, its bosses and bankers for various business ventures, and—above all—the beautiful receptionist at our hotel. Amal, as she was called, would become Abdel's wife. They have three children to date.

But, in the meantime, we returned to Marrakech, where we took up our winter quarters.

*

Clara,

My pain has emigrated to this beautiful city. I have survived by smoking, floating through the days, my mind at one with my unwanted body. The plumes of hashish smoke have extinguished any sense of loss and emptiness.

In the garden, the palm trees bow gently in the mild winter breeze. The air is crystalline and fresh; it feels wonderful inhaling it into my battered lungs. At one point a glimmer of light appeared in my charred memory. I stared at the desert and the dunes for a long time until a flicker ran through me like a ripple through the sand, and then I sank down into a new torpor.

I am ensconced on a café terrace and everything is a blur. Sometimes my eyes darken and I check out for a few moments, and when I come to, I see a face. The beautiful young women pass me by, surprised and a little worried. I try to make them stay with a smile. You're with them, I smile at you too. I let myself drift. Reality has no consistency here, it's wonderful. Everything is ambiguous, there's no sense of the moment. Distances contract, the present expands; every sort of rhythm, eternal and ephemeral, merges into one. The confusion is intoxicating. We meet in the clouds; I doze in the sun. I can't tell what's simultaneous from what's sequential. Everything's an approximation. It's not madness, though; if anything, it's just an easing off. As the pressure decreases, my distinguishing features fade away. Perhaps this is what freedom really is. I don't exist anymore, and so I am free. Limbo must be a state like this, where you lack everything.

Rose-Tinted City

A MARRAKECHI WOMAN ABSENTMINDEDLY stroked a foreigner's thigh. She seemed a sad creature, lost in remote fantasies. Were these beautiful people going to be spoiled by our wayward society? Every house had its disingenuous satellite dish.

Time hardly seemed to exist in Marrakech; chance meetings determined what I'd do next. Hours were spent in reveries in the shade of a palm tree, the future in God's hands. No need always to be snatching at the moment as it raced by. Inconsequential everyday events gave time its rhythm.

A stork climbed slowly through the lazy air.

*

I WONDERED if there was any way of sparing some people the worst of their suffering. What if everyone suffered equally under the mute, reproachful gaze of the gods? Could there ever be a time of universal healing? Who would want to be a martyr in an age without pain?

*

I ASKED women to stay with me, even though we couldn't talk, because their scent gave me sustenance. I sensed a glimmer of hope in the unpitying gaze of a child. His quizzical look was proof I existed. We gave each other a slight smile. I wanted to make his life easier in some way. How could anyone dare suggest that deprivation was all that awaited him? Frugality is a different matter.

*

I WONDERED whether I could love someone else without sinking back into the old turmoil. Could I survive in this lifeless desert where so many nomads had their graves? It felt as if many others had looked up like me at the washed-out blue of the sky. I shivered in the burning sun; scattered storks trailed across the sky; it wasn't too late.

*

THE LUSH clumps of bougainvillea, the scarlet waterfalls of climbing roses, the whisper of the ocher zellige fountain, the quivering olive trees—why couldn't these be the enchantments I saw every day? I could stop rebelling, finally.

Even as the thought formed, I hated myself for its complacency. How could I contemplate things becoming easier? I had to seek out dissonance. I had to dress and bandage the world. I had to be more compassionate, go into the slums to help the dying to their feet, provide shelter for the orphans, stanch the flow of rebels. I would dream among the faded sounds. At daybreak, strangers would stir and find me on lookout. Every day I would inspect the palette of injustice and choose the futile act that would bring me peace.

*

AND YET I still felt love. The urge toward the unknown drew me away from sadness. Every morning a beautiful woman with firm breasts passed my palm tree without glancing at me. If only she'd look up. . . . Once, I locked eyes with a Berber woman and stared intensely into her jade gaze until taboo and habit broke the connection. Another time, I said incoherent things to a somber redhead who moved away with a smile. The magic of women brought me relief.

*

I WOKE up lighthearted one morning and set out, feeling brand new. The beautiful Koutoubia mosque towered overhead. Eddies of dust flew up. Sorrow loosened its hold on me. I joined in the imam's prayer. The worshippers had spilled out of the mosque and were kneeling in the road. The beggars crouched and held out their hands, each reciting his chant. I watched the shoe-shine boy touting his presence with a *rat-tat* on his box. A wrinkled storyteller with a white beard drew a crowd. Occasionally someone would call out to him and raise a hand, a note between their fingers, and, as the ritual of expectation renewed itself, the crowd grew. A dozen blind old men chanted questioningly in unison, their eyes rolled back to the heavens. In a deep trance, the Gnawa repudiated their former slavery, the tassels of their taguia flapping jerkily like a flag of rebellion,[3] and the snake charmers kept time with them.

The sparrows and the pigeons whirled in and out of the dust and smoke from the grills. Water vendors poured glinting threads, as the bells on their broad, red hats struck the vibrating air. I felt good in that anonymous crowd. I was part of the dance and felt no remorse. I saw how to embed myself in the moment so I could be part of the structured chaos. I joined in the anonymous play of glances, let myself drift, weightless, on the swell, attuned to every indifference. Time had to be broken down into ever smaller sections, one second abandoned to plunge into the next, without regret or expectation, simply a sense of wonder at the fact of repetition. At last I felt I existed in my immobility, caught up in a new rhythm. I had erased all my memories: I had never been, I never would be again, I simply was, dense, instantaneous.

Nefertiti, goddess of the impossible, floated across the square; the women veiled themselves, the men wept.

*

---

3 Taguia: a hat worn by the Gnawa, a religious brotherhood descended from African slaves. They practice a syncretic rite of possession.

FOR THE first time in my blank memory, a light appeared behind my eyelids. I stared at the desert dunes and the haze of
the heat for a long time. I plunged into this new torpor, and
saw . . . I saw her. Not you.

*

Clara,
      An envelope in your beautiful writing has arrived.
Don't be angry with me anymore.

Lalla Khadīja

I SAW HER AS the crowd scattered for shelter from a sudden downpour. She floated across the square between the abandoned carriages and the panicky, whinnying horses. The avenue of palm trees bowed at her nonchalant passing. She seemed to glide, a slight figure, indifferent to the storm. The flags of the royal palace snapped in the wind. A ray of sunshine pierced the clouds, picking her out. A child held out its hand to her, then they both disappeared.

A few people ventured into the square; a blind man resumed his complaint. A water vendor cursed the rain. I must have dreamed that unlikely moment. A flash of grace had lit up the usual course of events. From that moment on, I waited for her to come back.

*

FEVER AND burning were shutting me off from everything. Worried by my reclusive silence, a friend invited me to her riad. I lay near the fountain on the patio. Long, cool fingers caressed my face; a melody carried me far away. When I looked up, the beauty with the child was coming up the alley, stepping between the skittish horses. Finally unveiling her smile, she said her name was Khadija; she had dark eyes. Her daughter Sabah's little hand rested on my fingers. "Hello," I smiled at her. "I'm your godfather."

A daughter of Egypt and Sudan, she had inherited her sloped profile from ancient bas-reliefs. She had found Sabah on the riverbank. With her long hands, she had woven sabri, the cactus silk of the desert, when she was kidnapped by an Almoravid king who died on the walls of Marrakech.

From then on, the beauty of the desert and the child of the river were at my bedside every day. I told stories to incredulous dark eyes. Sabah did not understand me, but she smiled anyway, and her mother would prompt her. I asked her to sing me a song. Sometimes I would recognize a French nursery rhyme and join in, mumbling the bits I remembered. Sabah would laugh. When she came back from school, she would show me her copybook in calligraphic Arabic script and in Latin characters. I congratulated her on her hard work. One day she asked me when I was going to get better. "It will take time. But you can help me."

Khadija sat her at a table to do some drawing, then took my hand. She didn't say anything at first, then gently rested her head on my painful shoulder. Her hand delicately brushed my cheek. I kissed her forehead and closed my eyes, inhaling her lemony scent. She fell asleep. I watched over her, moved by such a trusting nature. A ray of sunshine opened her eyes and she smiled at me and squeezed closer. We stayed like that, fragile and hopeful. She kissed me tenderly.

We went away to the shores of Lake Lalla Takerkoust. The eternal snows lay all around. Sabah swam, we drifted; fishing boats lazed in the distance, a few seagulls hovered idly overhead. God languished. I had erased Clara. Béatrice was luminous. Khadija drew me firmly down into the cool water.

I found an oasis of hundred-year-old olive trees at the foot of the Atlas Mountains, where I was going to build an adobe house to have the ones I love to stay. We would give lessons to ragged children from the neighboring *douar,* village.

They had become my companions.

The Odyssey

WIJDANE, MY LITTLE girl, is hooked onto my paragliding harness. The wing—the same one I had twenty years ago, sky blue and sunshine yellow—is spread out behind me on the parvis of the Château de la Punta. A warm breeze rises off the Gulf of Ajaccio.

"Shall we go, sweetheart?"

Khadija is standing to one side: "Be careful!"

"No problem," I reply in a very Abdelian way.

I move forward, the wing inflates above our heads, I apply a little brake, and we're off.

"Wijdane! Look at the buzzard soaring over there on the left. Shall we have a race?"

I angle the wing. Below, Béatrice is on the porch in her white, transparent dress and her straw hat with the fuchsia ribbon. She has been with me like this all these years. On her arm, a basket of roses from the garden.

Laetitia is pushing the stroller containing her youngest

child, who is shielded by a parasol. Sabah does not look up from her book. Robert-Jean bends down to his fiancée in the shade of the chestnuts in blossom. Below them is the tower and the funerary chapel.

We spin in a thermal. Wijdane bursts into peals of laughter.

"Life is crazy, darling. Life is wonderful!"

ESSAOUIRA, AUGUST 2011

Afterword

OLIVIER NAKACHE AND Éric Toledano, the directors of
the film *Intouchables* (2011), rang me up one day in January
2010. Years before, they had seen an hour-long documentary
directed by Jean-Pierre Devillers and produced by Mireille
Dumas. Titled *À la vie, à la mort* (*Through Thick And Thin*)
(2002), it told the unlikely story of how I, a rich and privileged quadriplegic, and Abdel, a young second generation
North-African from a housing project, met and helped each
other for many years. Our intrepid filmmakers were interested in adapting it for the screen. My wife Khadija and I
gave them lunch at our house in Essaouira, along with the
actors they were considering for the leads, Omar Sy and
François Cluzet. We saw one another repeatedly and it was
a delight following their script through each stage of its development.

The book that inspired the documentary, *Le second souffle*
(*A Second Wind*) (2001), which was out of print by then, had
received a certain amount of critical acclaim. Frédéric Boyer—

251

the editorial director of Bayard Éditions, my publishers—offered to republish it to coincide with the film's release and suggested I add a preface and a fresh installment to bring the story of my travails up to date. *The Guardian Devil,* therefore, picks up from where *A Second Wind* left off in 1988 and continues up to the point at which I met Khadija in Morocco in 2004, this being the time span covered by the script of *Intouchables.* The constraints of the film and their imaginations led the directors to simplify, change, cut, or invent many events.

"Untouchable" applied to both Abdel and me in a variety of ways. Abdel's North-African background meant he had always felt marginalized in French society, like an untouchable in India. If you did touch him, there was a high risk you'd get punched, and he was such a fast runner that the po-po, to use his expression, had only managed to nab him once in his long career as a delinquent.

As for me, sheltered behind the high walls of my Parisian town house—my gilded cage, as Abdel called it—wanting for nothing because of my money, I was one of the masters of the universe; nothing could touch me. Or so people thought. In fact, my total paralysis and loss of sensation prevented me from touching anything. Everyone was so terrified of my condition they hesitated even to brush against me, and if someone did touch my shoulder, it was horrifically painful.

Untouchables, then.

So there I was, confronted with an insane challenge, that of revisiting the past. One thing immediately became obvious to me: I couldn't remember it! At first I put this down to the fact that Abdel, my caregiver, wasn't with me anymore. But, on reflection, it proved more serious. Apart from unearthing a few episodes and being very hazy about dates, my memory refused to play along. Remembrance of things past is a luxury of the healthy and prosperous. When you're poor or sick, your memory concentrates on the here and now as you struggle to earn a living or stay alive. Only an upper-class dandy could become obsessed with Proust's madeleine.

It was the same when I was writing *A Second Wind* between 1998 and 2001. Wracked with grief—my wife Béatrice had only just died—and neuropathic pain, I said then how difficult it was to glue the fragments of my past back together.[4] Pain destroys one's memory. The healthy grow old storing up memories and regrets; my mind is as smooth as pumice, all my memories have been worn away.

An autobiography is bound to be full of things the author has misremembered or distorted, whether intentionally or by omission. But when you tell someone else's story, Abdel's in this case, the most you can do is give an impression of the other person, an outline with large areas left blank. How was I, the supposedly well-raised aristocratic

---

4 Neuropathic pain: roughly a third of quadriplegics suffer from neurological disorders, which result in phantom pain—particularly burning. Its intensity varies according to the individual, his or her condition, and climate. I hit the jackpot. For almost twenty years I have been oscillating between 6 and 9.5 on the pain scale. When you get to 10, it's "Thank You and Goodnight."

stickler for certain codes of behavior, meant to speak for someone like Abdel, who was in full-blown revolt when I met him and rejected rules of any kind? All I can do is say what happened and try to analyze it. Part of the truth about him still eludes me. Omar Sy, who plays him on screen, finds him much easier to fathom.

I wanted to write a book that wasn't simply an entertainment. I didn't want to create a "realistic" portrait of hardship with its prerequisite of resentment and more or less patronizing finer feelings, and I certainly wasn't going to go in for any fake optimism either, that pathetic lie.

These twenty years' exposure to the world of outcasts have made me more clear-eyed about society and its ills, so I wanted to set out a number of remedies that strike me as self-evident. My guardian devil Abdel has helped me to recover the sense of humor I used to have before the tragedies, and it's entirely appropriate that the film *Intouchables* is light and fast-moving and full of laughter. Nevertheless, I've been left with a certain irreducible seriousness at my core, which François Cluzet has been able to convey with his acting.

Éric and Olivier, the directors; Nicolas Duval Adassovsky, their producer; and Frédéric Boyer, my editor, have donated a generous share of their profits to Simon de Cyrène, the charity I have run for many years, which adapts apartments for adults with disabilities and their families and friends. I am very grateful to them.

I also wish to thank Émeline Gabaut, Manel Halib, and

my daughter Sabah, who allowed me to take up my pen again. This book would never have existed if it weren't for them. Thanks also to Soune Wade, Michel Orcel, Michel-Henri Bocara, Yves and Chantal Ballu, Max and Marie-Odile Lechevalier, and Thierry Verley, who read through the manuscript and made extremely pertinent comments.

THE SIMON DE CYRÈNE ASSOCIATION is a charitable organization based in France dedicated to providing apartments for adults with disabilities and their families and friends. Philippe Pozzo di Borgo, the author of *A Second Wind,* is a cofounder and honorary president of the organization. If you would like to learn more about the work of Simon de Cyrène or find out how to make a donation, please contact them at:

Simon de Cyrène
12 rue de Martignac, 75007 Paris
Telephone: 011 33 1 82 83 52 33
www.simondecyrene.org

About the Translator

Will Hobson's translations from French and German include the Goncourt Prize winner *The Battle* by Patrick Rambaud, *The Collector of Worlds* by Iliya Troyanov, and *Being Arab* by Samir Kassir, which won the Index on Censorship Freedom of Expression Award.